BIBLE BELT BLUES

Bible Belt Blues

COLLECTED ESSAYS

Hal Crowther

— BLAIR —

Blair is an imprint of Carolina Wren Press.

The mission of Blair/Carolina Wren Press is to seek out, nurture, and promote literary work by new and underrepresented writers.

We gratefully acknowledge the ongoing support of general operations by the Durham Arts Council's United Arts Fund and the North Carolina Arts Council.

Library of Congress Control Number: 2025029300

CONTENTS

FOREWORD

I t is my great pleasure to welcome you to *Bible Belt Blues,* the most incisive and original comment on our beloved and beleaguered Southland today, and to introduce you to its author Hal Crowther, who happens to be my husband. This does not mean that I understand how he does it, essay after essay on wildly divergent topics, often Southern, year after year. I don't even know *when* he does it, exactly. All I can say is, Hal is never *not* writing—that is, not reading, not thinking, not looking and listening . . . we receive a large number of actual newspapers and magazines, of course, spilling onto the floor, not to mention books, real books, now filling several rooms in this old house. Hal does not always work at a desk, he might be in his favorite armchair, in the kitchen, or on the porch. Whenever he gets ready to write a column, or an essay he just *does it*—first draft straight out of the computer, as far as I can tell—though I'm aware of how much thought and selection has clearly gone into it. All I can say is, it's an honor and a revelation to be here when it happens.

The topics are many, from the randy preachers in the title chapter to the equally randy elected officials in "Sex and the Southern Politician," the loss of history and the liberal arts in today's school curriculums, the reemergence of the Ku Klux Klan, the NRA and the need for gun control. But I am especially struck by Hal's prophetic writings about Trump in many of these essays. In "Dark Clouds Gathering: Homegrown Fascists Show Their Teeth," he writes, "Even Hitler had his friendly billionaires," followed by other disturbing parallels. I hope these relevant and entertaining essays will delight you, too.

—*Lee Smith*

BIBLE BELT BLUES

Introduction

A TRAIL OF TEARS?

For a collection of essays without an unmistakable, tightly wound theme, the author owes his readers a kind of road map, a well-marked path to reassure them that nothing they encounter is random or idle speculation. These essays were published over more than a decade of drastic changes and very real threats to nearly everything most of us hold sacred. What they represent is something like a brain scan of one veteran observer as he reacted to the heavy weather of the twenty-first century.

"Veteran" in this case is not a casual adjective. It's not a boast or a claim of legitimacy, but an unchallenged fact that this veteran has been paid for his published opinions for more than fifty-five years, in such a variety of publications that a list alone would unbalance this foreword. There are opinions and prejudices that have held steady over the years, a few that have been abandoned, and some recent ones every reader will quickly recognize. One of those is a profound distaste for social media. The fact that millions of the rankest, rudest, least responsible amateurs now dominate the American conversation—and nudge professional journalism toward extinction—causes excruciating pain among survivors of the Old Guard. Those of us who reached middle age before "internet trolls," "Twitter mobs," and "the attention economy" became a part of the national vocabulary are still bewildered and defensive. Who knew that half the human race nursed an aching void that could only be filled by constant communication and incontinent sharing?

The truth, as President Biden emphasized in his farewell warning against the disinformation industry, is not determined democratically, by numbers or by volume. And all opinions are not equal or worthy of the same respect. Your guess, in other words, is probably not as good as mine. In the twentieth century the American press—even that Gutenberg-haunted word sounds archaic—had achieved levels of professionalism and public trust that survived the Red Scare, the Vietnam War, and even the TV revolution. Editors I worked for in the sixties and seventies were determined to get the story right, and there was no place for you if you didn't share that commitment. But in the age of the internet much of that earned prestige has been lost, undermined by those armies of trolls, Fox News, alt-right radio, and an idiot president who calls journalists "the enemy of the people." One recent poll showed that the public's trust in "legacy media" had slipped below 30 percent.

The apparently unavoidable eclipse of my profession is a dark cloud that hovers over much of the work that's presented here. Another cloud that lingers is in the area of regional pride, or shame. I've been a voting citizen of the state of North Carolina for nearly half a century, which centers me strategically between the Old Blood Confederate (which I am not) and clueless hordes of new arrivals who settle here with no memories or knowledge of our history. I've seen some of the best—several generations of fair, moderate governors and congressional Democrats—and some of the worst: the Greensboro Massacre, the stubborn afterlife of the Klan, and Jesse Helms's seniority-fueled rampage through the United States Senate.

Our trends as I write this are not encouraging. Some of the most ruthless Republicans in the South's legislative menagerie have gerrymandered our best representatives out of Congress and made every effort to emasculate the reasonable governors we persist in electing. One of the lowest points in North Carolina's political history was achieved in the November 2024 election, when those uninhibited statehouse Republicans carefully groomed a weird reactionary, self-described as "a Black Nazi," and ran him for governor. Thank God he lost, but maybe only because working journalists exposed his lewd posts to a website called Nude Africa. In presidential elections, Tar Heels have slipped from a proud majority for Barack Obama in 2008 to three consecutive majorities for Donald Trump.

That name, Trump, which years ago I prayed I'd never have to type again, will be encountered many times in these pages. The name itself is like a fire bell in the night, and if you aren't frightened, you're not paying attention. The hulking primate who's attached to this name has cast a long shadow over the decade these essays encompass. He's not the cause, but more accurately the unlikely symbol of destructive changes in the collective mind of America. I wouldn't blame it all on social media. But twenty years ago anyone who predicted that Donald Trump would be a two-term president of the United States would have been dismissed as a madman or a cynic too savage to be credible.

As it happens, as I'm writing this, he's preparing to swear his second oath of office tomorrow—on Martin Luther King Day. Looking back over what I've written, I see that his first flash of interest in the presidency, back in 2012, was dismissed by me as a laughing matter, hard proof that the Republican Party had sunk below the waterline. Way back in 1996, in a collection titled *Unarmed But Dangerous*, I cited him as one of the most ridiculous celebrities who had ever caught America's attention. Since no one who admires or respects Mr. Trump will be likely to read this book, I address myself only to his detractors when I describe my approach to the forty-seventh president as more clinical than political. Key members of his first cabinet and several members of his extended family have warned us that he's mentally ill ("atomic crazy," writes his nephew), buttressed by the 225 psychiatrists and mental health professionals who signed a preelection letter to *The New York Times*, diagnosing him as a malignant narcissist in rapid cognitive decline. It concluded with this warning: "Without question, malignant narcissists have been history's most grandiose, paranoid and murderous leaders. Inevitably, they escalate until they are completely out of control, ultimately destroying themselves and the nations they lead."

Hail to the Chief. Writing about Trump and the MAGAfied Republican Party he has tamed and shamed, it's pointless to review the old ideological clashes between the free market economy and big government, etc., etc. For me the best analogy is oncological. "Malignant" is the ominous word. MAGA with its xenophobia and creeping fascism is a national cancer, and President Trump was a huge malignant tumor that indicated it might be fatal. When he was defeated and excised in 2020, the nation went into remission, full of hope. But four years later, as is often the case with this disease, we have suffered a crushing recurrence.

This president has no firm beliefs and no skills except self-promotion. If he's not the ultimate monster spawned by the attention economy and the "look at me" century, I don't want to live to see the creatures who might build on his tradition. Every change he promises us will be harmful. Some, like annexing Greenland and renaming the Gulf of Mexico, are simply insane. Others, like denying climate change and reversing environmental legislation, are genocidal. Most honest journalists treated Trump satirically until it became obvious that he defies all exaggeration. He has murdered satire as MacBeth murdered sleep. How can we attempt humor when what we want to do is weep?

And yet, through the span of years covered by the work in this book, Trump was not the most deadly disease we encountered—not yet the most deadly, at least. Arriving in his wake, at the end of his chaotic first term, was the international terror we named Covid-19. We lost friends and family members to this virus, we lost months of prime lifetime along with most of our sense of time. Covid changed everything forever, and it persists with new mutations and new warnings.

Long before the pandemic had begun to wane, Russia invaded Ukraine and Hamas committed the massacre that set the Middle East on fire, opening the possibility of world wars on two fronts. Global warfare coincided with global warming. Infernal heat waves caused thousands of deaths on every continent, as each year broke the world heat record that was set the year before. Wildfires raged, fueled by droughts, and school shootings multiplied in the U.S., even as politicians like Trump kissed the bloody trigger finger of the NRA.

Welcome to the twenty-first century. If it sounds like the Trail of Tears, don't blame me. These essays are separate responses to separate events, not a blueprint for despair. Critics have noted that "lighthearted" is not the prose tone where I'm most comfortable—though I was once introduced as a humorist at a reading in Florida. There are lighter moments in this collection. If my dark side is beginning to get you down, reader, try "Sex and the Southern Politician." And in the midst of our modern sorrows, what about the comforts of religion? They're not usually accessible to me, but I recommend the essay "Christian Soldiers," a eulogy for those warrior priests the brothers Berrigan, whom I deeply admired.

What I've attempted to gather here is a series of rational reactions to irrational forces. It's my fondest hope that my pleas for reason will not be mistaken for another version of the party line, another partisan pleading from a familiar position toward the left end of the political spectrum. By temperament I'm a lifelong nonaffiliate, one who has never joined or helped to fund a political party. But I think one of the saddest losses, in a nation as polarized as America today, is our flight from literate debate. In the Age of Trump, the Lincoln/Douglas tradition has been replaced by smears, lies, insults, adolescent name-calling. In the months ahead, many voices in the beleaguered media will attempt to sound evenhanded, as if the warring parties are equally responsible for the rapid decline of our democracy. This is pathetic. The white-power cartel that was once the Republican Party embraces demonic vermin like Alex Jones, who tormented the grieving parents of massacred schoolchildren. Dizzy with conspiracy theories, contaminated by the worst Americans and their worst ideas, the "GOP" has willfully excused itself from any coherent branch of the national conversation.

This is what I think. Feel free to disagree.

—Hal Crowther, Jan. 20, 2025

PART ONE

Old Times There Are Not Forgotten

Facing the Founder

ON A DAY OF SHAME

2021

One of the stranger things I might choose to boast about is that the grave of a Signer of the Declaration of Independence is virtually in my backyard. William Hooper's tombstone in the Old Town Cemetery of Hillsborough, North Carolina, lies just ten feet from my property line. Hooper (1742–1790), a member of the Continental Congress and one of three North Carolinians who signed the Declaration, was a Harvard-educated attorney who once cut a great figure in North Carolina, before and after the Revolution. His personal history is a colorful one that encompasses much of the drama, risk, and uncertainty of his time.

Here was a Founding Father, a man who must have known Washington, Jefferson, Franklin, and Hamilton, maybe even Thomas Paine. Born and educated in Boston, he certainly knew the Adamses. His grave is not frequently visited, not even by schoolchildren in this history-saturated town, but as his closest neighbor I've long been in the habit of paying my respects. And even, in times of great civic peril, of consulting Hooper symbolically. It's not easy to astonish a man my age who has spent more than a half-century in the news business. But after the mind-bending horrors of January 6 in Washington, where a lunatic president incited neo-Nazi thugs to trash the Capitol building and rout Congress, I took my astonishment and sorrow to that quiet corner of the Old Town Cemetery where Mr. Hooper was laid to rest.

"Well, where do we go from here, sir?" I asked, half out loud. It's necessarily a one-sided conversation with a gentleman who has been a ghost, at best, since 1790. And how could he understand that riots and insurrections, in 2021, are the evil offspring of social media? A concept like "Twitter mobs" would bewilder an eighteenth-century lawyer even more than it bewilders me. But that ancient weathered tombstone sent back more comprehension and sympathy than I could ever expect from Lindsey Graham or

Mike Pompeo. And without a doubt more useful legal advice than anyone could expect from Rudy Giuliani.

"What's next?" I pressed Hooper, a prosecutor who had served as deputy attorney general. "Trump's maniacs were screaming, 'Hang Mike Pence!'" And I swear I heard a spectral voice answer "Impeach! And convict."

The sad irony is that William Hooper knew all about mobs—and riots, and the personal disasters and humiliations that may befall patriots in times of upheaval. When he lived here, quiet, quaint Hillsborough was a focal point for the War of the Regulation (1765–1771), the pre-Revolutionary insurrection that some historians cite as the beginning of the end of British rule in America. As an officer of the Crown, Hooper was on what many would regard as the "wrong" side of that controversial affair. When the Regulators rioted in Hillsborough in 1770, he and several other lawyers and officers of the court were seized physically and dragged through the streets.

Hooper was with the colonial militia, commanded by Governor William Tryon, when it dealt the Regulators their final defeat at the Battle of Alamance in 1771. Presumably he was present when Tryon, known during the approaching Revolution as an exceptionally brutal British general, hanged six of the Regulator leaders on a hill near the Hillsborough courthouse. Ten years later, when Hooper was pursued as a fugitive for his role in the Continental Congress, British troops came to Hillsborough and burned his home. I can see that rebuilt colonial structure, now occupied by a retired cardiologist, from the window where I'm sitting.

Several other Signers were tortured to death by the British, atrocities that are not common knowledge. After the riot at the Capitol last week, some of the congressional idiots who encouraged it referred to January 6 as "a 1776 moment," implying that the savage rabble stalking Trump's "enemies" were patriots who will be remembered like the Boston Tea Party or Paul Revere. That's laughable from a dozen angles. But only people like Hooper, who lived through it, could explain how complicated the actual 1776 moment must have been.

The descent from George Washington to Donald Trump is so precipitous that it's hard to imagine without vertigo, without nosebleeds. Without tears. But one thing that never changes is the nature—the deplorable human nature—of mobs. They've been with us always, congregations of cowards who feed off each other's ignorance and rage. More than a century after the death of William Hooper, H. L. Mencken surveyed American democracy and was not charmed. He's rarely more eloquent than when he's sneering at what he calls "the eternal mob-man."

"Behind all the great tyrants and butchers of history he has marched with loud hosannas, but his hand is eternally against those who seek to liberate the spirit of the race.... In two thousand years he has moved an inch: from the sports of the arena to the lynching party," Mencken wrote in "Notes on Democracy." And in the same vein, "Public opinion, in its raw state, gushes out in the immemorial form of the mob's fears. It is piped to central factories, and there it is flavored and colored, and put into cans."

The mob with its violent potential is always there, like a crater lake of gasoline where only the most desperate, unhinged demagogue would dare to throw a match. On January 6 we saw what happens when one dares. The North Carolina Regulators had a great deal more to rage about than the Trumpist Neanderthals who invaded the Capitol, but we see disturbing similarities in their behavior. In the Hillsborough riots of 1768 a Regulator mob vandalized the provincial courthouse, leaving excrement on the judge's chair and a decomposing corpse on the lawyers' bench. Regulators dragged officials through the streets and threatened to lynch them, beat one lawyer so badly that he lost an eye, and burned the house of the presiding judge and dozens of other buildings. They literally left Hillsborough in ruins and in flames.

It wasn't pretty, and it wasn't genteel. The only thing that made me laugh—bitterly—about the events of January 6 was an eyewitness report that Trump, the lowest lowlife (as a grown man with children, he was the favorite guest on Howard Stern's infantile sex-talk show) who ever occupied the White House, watched the riot on TV and enjoyed everything except the fact that his murderous vandals were so obviously "low-class." He had intuited that the bearded thugs in horned helmets and "Camp Auschwitz" T-shirts weren't Ivy Leaguers or investment bankers.

Mobs are always the same. But what has changed, lethally, in the age of technology and new media is the way they're organized, mobilized, and sustained. In Hooper's day the mob-men, in order to meet and reinforce each other's worst prejudices and wildest impulses, were obliged to walk, ride, or steer horse-drawn vehicles over miles of muddy roads. In the age of Trump the Twitter troll, they scheme and foment and concoct wild conspiracy theories on social media (a headline in today's *New York Times*: "How Facebook Incubated the Insurrection"). The internet has become such a

separate dimension and such a fecund breeding ground for racist nostalgia and malignant political fantasy that its wired mobs can escape reality
altogether. They've become the foot soldiers every demagogue and dictator most covets, as the philosopher Hannah Arendt explained in "The Origins of Totalitarianism (1951): "The ideal subject of totalitarian rule is not
the convinced Nazi or the convinced Communist, but the people for whom
the distinction between fact and fiction (i.e., the reality of experience) and
the distinction between true and false (i.e., the standards of thought) no
longer exist."

This erosion of the actual, this contemptuous dismissal of the very idea
of "truth" may prove to be the most toxic legacy of the serial liar Donald
Trump. Twisted and inflated in the spookiest corners of the internet, his
shameless lies will spur mobs and smother common sense long after the
last rude scratch on our Capitol building has been repaired. There are many
things I could never explain to a Founding Father like Mr. Hooper, who
predated the Industrial Revolution. But as a well-educated man at a time
when they were uncommon, he would have been well acquainted with feral stupidity. Would he have encountered enough of it to comprehend the
twenty-first-century bloodguilt cult called QAnon, which seems to have seduced enough cognitively impaired Americans to merit front-page coverage in the national media? Millions, they claim?

QAnon is a comic-book Otherworld where the superhero Donald Trump
is the nation's last defense against a secret order of Satan-worshipping pedophiles and child-killers—suspiciously including many prominent Democrats and Jews—who actually rule the world. This bouillabaisse of psy-
chedelic paranoia is an infallible litmus test for morons. If you respond to
QAnon fantasies with anything short of hysterical disbelief, you are such
a cognitive shipwreck of a human being that no amount of training could
prepare you to compete with the average chimpanzee. At least two new Republican congresswomen have tested positive for QAnon.

Would the American experiment end as it began 250 years ago in Orange County, North Carolina, with bloodthirsty mobs rampaging through
public buildings? Can we move forward with Covid-19 devastating the nation's lungs and QAnon attacking its brains? But in desperate times, Mr.
Hooper might have tried to reassure me, remarkable people step forward.
The Founders had Washington to lead, they had Paine and Jefferson to
frame their thinking, and they prevailed. As I took my graveside leave of
Mr. Hooper, with the inauguration looming and threats of more armed ri-

ots, I was not confident at all. God bless President Biden. But I wouldn't want to be in his shoes.

Historical footnote: Even a Signer isn't guaranteed a final resting place. A century after his death, what remained of William Hooper was disinterred and reburied at the Guilford Courthouse National Military Park near Greensboro, where he has a statue. But I'm certain that his spirit remains here where he lay for years, yards from the house where he lived.

A Confederacy of Dunces?

ONCE AGAIN, DIXIE WANTS OUT

2021

I f you had any last lingering doubts about the desperate state of the Union, you haven't seen the results of a recent poll of Republican voters by Bright Line Watch/YouGov. Nationwide, 50 percent of the sample said they preferred secession to compromise with a Democratic administration. Among Southern Republicans—in the eleven states of the Old Confederacy plus Oklahoma and Kentucky—secession prevailed by a vote of two to one. Sixty-six percent of these patriots would be ready to fire on Fort Sumter once again. It's much the same nasty crowd that turned its guns on the United States in 1861. Back then they started a civil war so they could continue to buy and sell African slaves. This time they only want to keep those slaves' descendants from voting, or winning Senate seats. But it's a damn frightening echo, and it completes a repulsive descent into white supremacy for a Republican Party that once defeated those slaveholders and freed their slaves. This is no laughing matter. The most rabid of the GOP's congressional attack dogs, like Madison Cawthorn and Marjorie Taylor Greene, have allowed the infantile whimpering of a defeated, demented president to lure them to the brink of treason. If the statue-smashers are still punishing dead Confederate generals for betraying their country in 1861, what's a loyal American's response to red-state legislators who promote insurrection and secession in 2021? The gallows and the firing squad may be out of fashion, but aren't treason and sedition still serious crimes? Yet unsurprisingly, 40 percent of Democratic voters in the same Bright Line survey responded, essentially, "Let the bastards go."

My friend Gene Nichol, a distinguished constitutional scholar, now calls Republicans "the most dangerous anti-democracy party in the world." "The GOP has abandoned the American experiment," Nichol wrote in *The Progressive Populist*. "They now wage war against it. They seek to do what the Confederates couldn't. No wonder they're attached to the Stars and Bars.

The Republican Party has become home to moral, political, scientific, racial, democratic, and constitutional nihilism. It giddily embraces the destruction of our foundational norms and institutions. It cowers before our darkest forces, assuming it's safe to ride the back of the tiger."

No laughing matter. On one internet site that analyzes the secession survey, there's a photo of some Proud Boy thug parading the Confederate flag through the Capitol last January 6. If that doesn't chill you, friend, you're carrying the wrong passport. This is, as Nichol asserts, as serious as death—the death of an estimable democracy. But humor intrudes, rudely, when we try to imagine what kind of sovereign state would take its place on the world stage if our Southern Republicans were able to secede from this Union they profess to despise.

When any nation breaks apart—think about the Balkans and the former Yugoslavia—inevitably one of the divorced partners gets the best of what the former nation had to offer, and the other gets—the rest. The division of America along red/blue party lines would yield a spectacularly uneven divorce. It doesn't take much research to predict a demographic trainwreck for some new lily-white nation that would begin where America ends. Genetic diversity would be the first casualty, of course. White power would be such a universal assumption in an all-Republican principality that every non-white citizen in his or her right mind would pack a bag and light out for the cool blue north. There'd be no more work for Jim Crow or the KKK in the land where they used to flourish. In a few years this orphan nation would be whiter than Norway or Finland. The whitest but not the brightest of new nations, our red-state spin-off. The rest of its profile is all too predictable. By any measure of educational or intellectual achievement—test scores, high school graduates, college degrees, ranked universities, illiteracy—states dominated by Trumpublicans rank at or near the bottom of the American barrel. That's with the worst yet to come, once the divorce is finalized. The Republican Right's relentless war on science and medicine would soon cost the new polity most of its scholars, physicians, and scientists, those professionals who have always been the cream of the intellectual crop in a region where learning is undervalued. Professors and doctors would quickly follow minority Southerners on their northward migration, with engineers, high-tech industries, and the people who invest in them close behind.

It doesn't seem far-fetched to imagine a new Dark Age in Dixie, once secession detached it from the mainstream of Western civilization. Check those color-coded maps of America and you'll see that dark red states are already far behind the rest of the republic in critical categories like public health, poverty, and technology. They're suffering from more Covid cases and deaths, more vaccine resistance and fewer available ICU beds (none in Alabama) than any of the states that rejected Donald Trump. Those maps show that scarlet-red states lead the nation in only two demographic areas, each problematic—gun ownership and passionate Christianity.

Can you think of an unemployed demagogue, possibly an ex-president, who would not be embarrassed to take command of a nation of armed white Christians who can barely read? (Don't accuse me of exaggeration unless you're fully aware of what it means to rank in the intellectual subbasement of twenty-first-century America. According to the Organization for Economic Cooperation and Development, 50 percent of American adults are unable to read a book written at an eighth-grade level. Though the average American adult is a seventh-grade reader, watching Fox News requires an eleventh-grade level, according to the National Literacy Institute. Where the Old Confederacy raised its statues to native generals nicknamed "Old Hickory" and "Stonewall," will the New Confederacy raise them to a chubby draft dodger they call "Old Bone Spurs"?

I struggle to picture an equestrian statue like the one of General Lee on Monument Avenue in Richmond, complete with a horse that looked big enough to carry Doughy Donald. Would they set him on a throne in Birmingham, crown him president-for-life in Little Rock? No absurdity seems impossible, in these states that have shown so little resistance to Donald Trump's lies and fantasies. But the leadership of this post-American fragment state isn't one most generals or politicians would envy. Texas, the largest and most prosperous of the old Confederate states and one that harbors many ardent secessionists, has emerged as America's most radical opponent of abortion rights. The Texas statute that will soon face Supreme Court review—especially creepy because it adopts the fascist stratagem of inviting citizens to spy and inform on each other—is clearly this century's most ominous challenge to *Roe v. Wade.*

In a postsecession South, the Texas abortion ban would almost certainly become the law of the land. And, as an obvious consequence, nearly all the young women who lived in these red states would leave them for a saner reproductive environment—followed closely, in the course of nature, by all the young men. The average age of a Trumpland citizen might end up somewhere in the late fifties, which would eventually produce a terminal society of women too old to breed and men too old to fight. Even trou-

bled Mexico, eyeing this armed but decrepit society on its northern border, might revive the spirit of Pancho Villa and decide that it looked like
an easy conquest. I hope I'm not discouraging any of you eager secessionists, but there's one more demographic humiliation I feel compelled to
pass along. Obesity, as we all know, is a national pandemic that may end
up killing more Americans than Covid-19. And of course nine of the ten
most obese states (excepting only Michigan) are among those red states
that polled 2-to-1 for secession. The fattest five are Mississippi, West Virginia, Arkansas, Tennessee, and Kentucky. Donald Trump might fare better
running for president of the USA than taking the helm of a comic-book
nation that's predominantly old, white, sick, fat, and ignorant. Imagine
its Olympic team? In a Southern culture where sports have always been
fanatically central, shuffleboard would replace football and the hundred-
yard dash might take five minutes

A national motto for such a laughably unpromising republic might well
be borrowed from Dante's Hell: "Abandon hope all ye who enter here." I've
entertained myself trying to think of an appropriate name for a remote,
hopeless country where benighted gnomelike primitives live primitive lives.
In the funny pages, Al Capp of *Li'l Abner* fame invented Lower Slobbovia,
and the *Dilbert* cartoonist Scott Adams weighed in with a similar dystopia
he calls Elbonia. The novelist Gary Shteyngart coined "Absurdistan." After reviewing a number of humorous alternatives, some submitted by droll
readers ("Zombia," "Doofusland"?), I decided to call the New Confederacy "Oblivia." That would make its citizens "Oblivians," and anything con-
nected to this sad, poor land could be described as "Oblivious."

You might think I'm having too much fun with a subject as deadly serious as secession, or even suspect that I'm among the 40 percent of progres-
sives whose response to the South's secession movement is "good riddance."
Unfortunately I live in North Carolina, a state from the Old Confederacy
that has often been described as "purple" rather than red or blue, at least
since Barack Obama won its electors in 2008. But lately that purple has
been stained a dismal shade of pink. Obama lost North Carolina in 2012 and
Donald Trump prevailed there in 2016 and 2020. We have a Texas-size
problem with a Republican legislature that includes one infamous cretin—a
parson—who compared Abraham Lincoln to Adolf Hitler. (The late great
Molly Ivins referred to these feral legislators as "right-wing fruitloops," and
wouldn't it break her heart to see what the fruitloops and a looped-in gov-

ernor have wrought in her beloved Texas?) Carolina, as we call it—South Carolina is another world—has way more than its share of fruitloops, and our congressional delegation features the unspeakable Madison Cawthorn, whose antics leading up to January 6 may yet land him in the penitentiary.

Cry, the beloved country. Am I too old to emigrate? If worst truly comes to worst, in a replay of 1861, will North Carolina be consigned to Oblivia?

Bad News from Home

THE WHITE KNIGHTS RIDE AGAIN

2019

S ometimes coincidence and irony are so closely aligned that it's almost possible to believe in an omnipotent stage manager somewhere, someone with a wry smile on his face who moves all the pieces around just to amuse himself and bewilder the rest of us. If you're skeptical, I don't blame you. But try this. Last week in Maine I picked up the Arts section of *The New York Times* and found, in the daily recommendations column, a play opening at the Flea Theater, an off-Broadway venue in downtown Manhattan. This play, titled *Sincerity Forever*, is described as a satire of the Ku Klux Klan in a fictional Southern town. The playwright, Mac Wellman, has long been one of the mainstays of experimental theater in the city, an avant-garde celebrity—"notorious" or "distinguished" according to your taste—whose forty-odd plays include *Seven Blowjobs* (1991). The fictional Southern town where Wellman sets *Sincerity Forever* is named Hillsbottom, which scarcely caught my attention or provoked a smile when I looked up the play's history online. (It was described as a satire on "the indestructible nature of ignorance.") Two hours later, my email began to fill up with alarms and cell phone photos from neighbors in my hometown of Hillsborough, North Carolina. The trigger for their alarm, a spectacle quickly picked up by social and national media, was a Ku Klux Klan rally in front of the Orange County courthouse, two blocks from the house where I've lived for years.

There they stood, twenty-odd authentic white supremacists, some of them actually wearing their robes and pointed hoods, lined up along Churton Street where we walk every day. Four of them were holding up a large bedsheet sort of sign that read, "Help Make America Great Again, join the Loyal White Knights of the Ku Klux Klan." That's right—MAGA.

The embarrassment is intense, the personal response a major challenge. Of course a friend in Southern California emailed his sarcastic sympathy: "Are your neighbors planning a nice cross-burning for Labor Day?" A humorous reply didn't seem appropriate. The challenge is to defend Hillsbottom—excuse me, Hillsborough—without sounding too defensive. North Carolina's image has taken a beating lately, with our Republican legislators' "bathroom" bill to fend off the transsexual menace, and Trump trolls in Greenville shrieking "Send her back!" to gratify the smirking president who stokes their incoherent aggression. Tar Heel country is no peaceable kingdom. Like most Southern states these dark days, we harbor a visible minority of Trump-loving, race-baiting white cretins who have been getting the signal that their hour has come. But a Klan rally just one firm five-iron from my front yard?

Sneer if you will, but a Klan sighting is no more common, no more predictable in Hillsborough than it might be in Jersey City or Palo Alto. Mac Wellman's Hillsbottom is described as a "dirt-poor" Southern town. Our tasteful, "historic" Hillsborough, functioning capital of North Carolina during the American Revolution, is a low-profile community of old white frame houses, many of them dating from the eighteenth century, and old redbrick commercial buildings leased to restaurants and art galleries. Built along the Eno River where it crossed the Great Indian Trading Path, it was once a mill town, but the mills closed long ago. When it attracts attention, which is rarely, Hillsborough is noted as the home of an unusual number of writers, artists, and musicians, as well as faculty from Duke and the University of North Carolina at Chapel Hill. These residents tend to be liberals. Registered Democrats outnumber Republicans nearly 3-to-1 in Hillsborough, and the village has elected a Black mayor and a significant number of African Americans to local offices. Among the many historical markers along our main street are signs honoring the Black jazz composer Billy Strayhorn and the emancipated slave Elizabeth Keckly, who became Mary Todd Lincoln's dressmaker and closest confidante. Social events, even in private homes, are noticeably integrated, at least since I moved to the village in the mid-nineties.

A hotbed of white nationalism and retro-racism we are not, and never have been. Our mayor, Tom Stevens, a painter, quickly made it clear to gathering reporters that the Klansmen at the courthouse were not local—they had driven down from Rockingham County, fifty miles away—and not welcome. So why us, Loyal White Knights? Why were you practically standing on my lawn?

In modern North Carolina, sleepy old Hillsborough is nowhere near the

epicenters of political controversy or media attention. But the history of
our current collision with the Klan, as I understand it, is disturbing and
symptomatic of life in a bipolar America where Neanderthals are never far
away. White men carrying Confederate flags began appearing in Hillsborough several years ago when the village elders voted to remove the words
"Confederate Memorial" from the local history museum. According to my
neighbor Steven Petrow, writing in *The Washington Post*, the confrontation
heated up when the local chocolatier offered free chocolates to anyone who
would burn a Confederate flag. The chocolate maker received death threats,
Petrow reports, and the racist Right has had Hillsborough in its rifle sights
ever since.

My community's response to the Klan rally might be described as truly
inspiring: A week later citizens joined in a March Against Hate, parading
down King Street to the courthouse in intense late-August heat to hear a bi-
racial slate of speakers denounce the White Knights and all they stand for.
I wouldn't have expected anything less. But depression lingers. Even in a
backsliding country where various flavors of "alt-right" bigotry pose as patriotism and conservatism, the Ku Klux Klan with its long loathsome history of murder and terrorism remains a special case. To see men in Klan
hoods waving a banner with a slogan copyrighted by the president of the
United States is terrifying. To see them waving Confederate and American
flags side by side, as they did in Hillsborough, would be hilarious if it wasn't
so ominous. Do any of these hooded morons understand that the men who
flew the Southern Cross and the Stars and Bars were traitors, passionate
committed traitors, to the Stars and Stripes? You can't mix those flags. How
have our schools failed anyone so badly that we can still produce pseudo-
Confederates and Klansmen in 2019?

I guess we don't need a Yankee smart aleck like Mac Wellman to tell us
that ignorance is toxic and eternal. But I imagine I've seen more Klan rallies than Wellman has—I've seen two or three—and they were memorable
for the mixture of emotions they provoke. Anger and fear, of course, but
also pity. The last time I saw the Klan march, maybe twenty years ago in
the college town of Chapel Hill, it was a pitiful spectacle. Their fearsome
ranks amounted to a dozen bedraggled adults, who according to one reporter (me) seemed to have about twenty good teeth among them, and an
auxiliary of four or five half-starved children. You'd feel very sorry for them,
if they weren't armed and dangerous racist idiots. At the risk of class condescension, I'd classify these Klan warriors as the kind of rock-bottom pe-

rennial losers who define "the elite" as people with jobs. Imagine a life so empty of accomplishment or satisfaction that you find nothing to be proud of but your skin.

The Republican Party, which owes most of its recent electoral success to the loyalty of these incorrigibles and unteachables, no longer recognizes the term "white trash," which in the old South was an epithet every bit as stinging as the "N-word." The Klan, of course, has always had its own definition of "white." It's not just African Americans, Asian Americans, and Native Americans who fail to make the cut—Jews and Catholics aren't quite white enough either. The United States has such a rich racist tradition that it's kind of disingenuous to profess shock and horror when a few undernourished Klansmen take to the streets. The glorification of the "Nordic" race, complete with the pseudoscience to prove its superiority, has a fancy pedigree in America. Adolf Hitler and Heinrich Himmler both professed their admiration for the relentlessly anti-Semitic Henry Ford and for the blueblood eugenicist Madison Grant (1865–1937), author of the bestselling *The Passing of the Great Race* (1916). This upper-class racism was very much mainstream in their day. It's wise to avoid the personal letters of some of your favorite writers from those generations. Scott Fitzgerald and Henry Adams are two who recently disappointed me.

It's easy to see why poor white people feel marginalized and alienated, and furious when sober voices point out their pathetic, illogical allegiance to a party controlled by a billionaire class that ruthlessly sucks up every last nickel of America's wealth. It's not so easy to see why their bitterness and wrath are so easily redirected toward minority scapegoats, and anyone whose race, culture, or religion is different from their own. This is where the ancient pathology begins. What exactly are Klansmen marching for, what are they trying to say? In my profession there's a profound and necessary commitment to the First Amendment, and I'm uncomfortable when college censors of the liberal persuasion cite student "safety" as an excuse to ban crazy ultraconservative speakers. I think a campus evening with Richard Spencer or Ann Coulter might serve as a valuable class in abnormal psychology, and provide a few guilty laughs as well. But pure racism, the raw snarling kind practiced by the Klan, doesn't mix with free speech. It's mental illness. It rules out dialogue. What can anyone say to damaged people whose religion is hatred? What the fat fool in the White House has been saying to them, loud and clear, is "I'm with you." They wear their MAGA hats. What the fool doesn't understand—along with history, psychology, constitutional law, and climate science—is the destructive potential of those fires he's feeding. When a committed white nationalist like Steve Bannon can run a presidential campaign and serve as "chief strategist" for the president, the fragile membrane between "civilized," ideological, think-tank racism and the violent kind that breeds Klansmen and mass killers is wearing very, very thin. Four decades ago in North Carolina, I watched a news video of Klan killers shooting left-wing demonstrators at point-blank range. Five of them died, including two Ivy-educated physicians. None of the killers were ever convicted.

That wasn't in Hillsborough, but in Greensboro, just forty miles down Route I-40. They called it the Greensboro Massacre. We've come a long way since then, I thought until recently. Please don't come to Hillsborough for the cinematic thrill of seeing Klansmen in their robes. We've scared them off for now, I think. But most of the freaks you need to be afraid of don't wear hoods and robes. Look around carefully. Some fires are burning out of control.

A Whiter Shade of Pale?

2017

Dylann Roof's slaughter of elderly Black Christians in Charleston, as they prayed and beseeched him to put down his gun, ranks as one of the most hideous hate crimes ever committed by a single white supremacist—and one of the most irrational and inexplicable, as well. "What was he thinking?" is a question no sane person can ever answer, and nothing he said at his murder trial sheds much light in that direction. The death penalty is an archaic form of legal revenge I don't endorse under any circumstances, but the execution of a sad creature like Roof creates a formidable logical impasse. If this boy isn't insane, who and what can ever be judged insane, and how can we pretend to determine where madness begins?

A country that doesn't classify Dylann as a madman invites suspicion that its basic assumptions are unhinged. Slavery produced and nurtured a racist pseudoscience, a theology almost, that began with economic rationalization and hardened over the centuries into what appears to be hereditary mental illness, one that still disfigures and disables tens of millions of white Americans. The Charleston church murders were so disgusting, so nauseating in their blind cruelty that they resist generalizations. There may not be another Dylann Roof out there waiting to load his gun. A racist killing that was heartrending on a more intimate scale occurred on the University of Maryland campus last week, when a bowling alley attendant named Sean Urbanski ran—screaming—up to Richard W. Collins III and stabbed him fatally with a four-inch blade. Collins, an ROTC cadet who was about to graduate from Bowie State University and join the army as a second lieutenant, was African American. Urbanski, who is white, turned out to be a member of a Facebook group that called itself "Alt-Reich: Nation." (Other members of the group claim that they are satirists, not white supremacists.) Lt. Collins maintained a Facebook presence as well. *The New York Times* found something he posted in 2014: "I love all people and hate ignorance but I myself am ignorant so I am still working on loving all people."

On May 20 Richard Collins's pursuit of universal love was terminated by a white madman with a knife. He stopped trying to love us all, and went, we hope, to a much better place. Where the one certain thing is that he'll never meet another white supremacist. What are we supposed to do about these people, these rabid children of Hate and Ignorance whose very existence is a deadly poison in America's bloodstream? With the best of intentions it's a struggle to love thy neighbor, as the late Lt. Collins discovered. But how many more Black people need to die like this before Black people decide that every white neighbor is a threat to their survival? What then? I—white—feel no closer kinship to Dylann Roof or Sean Urbanski than Barack Obama might feel to Idi Amin. Yet every racial stereotype begins with some dreadful individual, some actual case, and every time that stereotype is reinforced the prejudice multiplies.

Black racism, in other words, is based on some all-too-accurate observations. It's a logical reaction—at worst an overreaction—to bitter experience. White racism is based on nothing but guilt, fear, and a profound misunderstanding of the whole human experience up to this point. If racism of both colors is intensifying just as it ought to be diminishing, there's nothing ahead of us, as Americans, but civil strife and violent decline. As someone wrote years ago, the United States of America has a café-au-lait future or no future at all.

When you encounter the word "white" attached to any organization or identity group—or the words "Caucasian" or "Aryan"—run as fast as you can in the opposite direction. Here comes Satan, in one of his most familiar American disguises. He doesn't quit easily. A century and a half has passed since Africans became citizens, and the sickness that afflicts their former enslavers is still an epidemic. The ruling party in Washington is a white people's party—there's no point in denying it—and it wins national elections by pandering to a "Solid South" of white Republicans who used to be Dixiecrat segregationists. The White House is occupied by a clueless racist, a former "Birther" who called Barack Obama a Muslim from Kenya, and his "chief strategist" used to manage the Breitbart website so dear to white supremacists and "alt-right" neofascists; the president's attorney general, who replaced an African American, is an ex-senator from Alabama whose racist reputation once cost him a seat on the federal bench.

It's not surprising, in this climate, that yet another crazy white man (they're nearly always men) felt encouraged to leave a noose in front of the KKK exhibit at the new National Museum of African American History and Culture in Washington. The museum's founder and director, historian Lonnie Bunch, reported in the *Times* that it was the third noose found at the Smithsonian Museums this spring. Others, Bunch reminded us, have been placed at Duke and American Universities, and inside a high school in Missouri. What this means, he concluded in an anguished op-ed essay, is that "we must lay to rest any notion that racism is not still the great divide."

His mention of the noose at Duke hits closer to home in North Carolina, where a series of cringe-making incidents have made us defensive, too quick to remind scornful liberals that more than half of us voted for Obama in 2008, and nearly half in 2012. There are a lot of decent white people in North Carolina. There are a lot of the others, too, and this year they think they're getting a green light from Washington. The Ku Klux Klan, which had fallen on hard times in the Carolinas, marched back into the news with a rally, dinner, and cross burning in Asheboro, home of our state zoo. I wish I could ask the animals what they think of Darwin-defying humans draped in Klan robes and hoods. In Raleigh, a belligerent crowd of Tea Party ya-hoos carried the Confederate flag and a Trump flag side by side. The worst of our wretched crop of Republican legislators, an astonishing idiot named Larry Pittman who's also a Baptist minister, made national news in April with a Facebook posting comparing Abraham Lincoln to Adolf Hitler.

The ghost of Jesse Helms still walks these hills. But the North Carolina news item that depressed me most of all came from Leesville Road Middle School in Raleigh, where three male students were suspended for another social media atrocity, a hardcore racist video that featured them chanting "KKK," "KKK" to punctuate a rant that would shame David Duke: "If you're in America, we don't accept niggers, Jews, Arabs, or pics. Go back to the fields of Alabama. Go back to the factories in Mississippi. You don't deserve freedom."

These are middle school students—thirteen, fourteen?—which accounts for the absence of logic, history, or geography. But their intent is clear, and the shock factor is their age. I'm not sure it's possible to reeducate adolescents with brains turned so rotten, so soon. The kindest way to end such wasted lives is to euthanize the poor kids, right now. They offer the community no value, civic or genetic. But if that seems harsh, maybe a wise judge would order them air-dropped in Boko Haram country in Nigeria, where they would either die in the first half-hour or learn, perhaps, that even African Muslim terrorists can behave more honorably than middle-school racists.

It's doubtful that any of the Leesville Three will ever matriculate, but if one of them should, he might find kindred spirits on many college campuses. A college printer at Vanderbilt University, apparently hacked, stunned the administration with a press run of anti-Semitic literature; the College Republicans of Central Michigan University disavowed a Hitler-themed Valentine's Day card that turned up among their brochures. The Anti-Defamation League, which began tracking campus hate groups last September, reports white supremacist recruiting efforts at sixty-six schools in thirty-two states.

"In a political environment where white supremacists have felt more welcome than at any time in recent memory, we saw them move from the margins to the mainstream," observed the League's director, Jonathan Greenblatt. The proliferation of racist hate groups since the election of Barack Obama is an old story—the Southern Poverty Law Center now lists nearly a thousand—but 2016, the year of Donald Trump, was a banner year for the Rabid White Right. Assessing the impact of the new president and his henchman Steve Bannon, Mark Potok of the Intelligence Report confirmed that "2016 was an unprecedented year for hate." And apparently the creeping chill of intolerance reaches children even younger than those middle-school videographers. A horrified elementary school counselor in Florida told a reporter, "An African-American child was asked if she was ready for shackles because she was going back to Africa. With tear-filled eyes she asked me: 'Can Donald Trump really do that?' We had a group of boys telling Latin American children to pack their things because they were going back to Mexico."

How are we supposed to live with people who condone such things and, worse yet, teach them to their children? America has accepted and assimilated people of every race and religion, but these homegrown palefaced bigots, deaf to reason and disfigured by hatred, may be the one minority the melting pot can never render. A disgrace to the white race and a threat to everyone else, they provide the breeding stock for the psychotic killers, vigilantes, bullies, and internet "trolls" who threaten to make the USA a nation where no one will want to live, if this vicious trend continues. Solutions? For anyone actually convicted of a hate crime, the option of quick, painless, merciful euthanasia, to remove them from their torment and from the gene pool. For the others, I support forced relocation to some of these expendable states that harbor so many white racists already—with an open invitation to secede from the Union.

I don't limit my Final Solution to those ugly, dangerous, mean-as-snakes crackers who join the Klan or hang out in Nazi chat rooms. We need to get rid of their middle-class auxiliary, too, those seersucker "Christian" hypocrites who vote for the same god-awful politicians to save a buck on their taxes or protect their property values. A more drastic approach would be expedited emigration to some pale monochromatic nation—Iceland, Finland?— where no one's pigmentation could ever offend them again. That is, if there's any society that would welcome the dregs of America, which I doubt. Call my solutions ethnic cleansing, if you like, but my only goal is the greatest good for the greatest number of American citizens.

This may sound as if I'm satirizing the overheated rhetoric of right-wing media, but don't mistake exaggeration for insincerity. I'm at a stage of exasperation that threatens my health. When I open the morning paper and find a photograph of the white supremacist Fuhrer Richard Spencer (dressed in a white suit, with a Confederate flag flying behind him) shaking hands in front of the Lincoln Memorial . . . the Lincoln Memorial! When I see this smiling troll in his designer sunglasses, my exasperation hardens into despair. Is it unreasonable to think that even minimal education could have produced a post-racial American society by the twenty-first century? Instead, it's Springtime for Hitler, for Richard Spencer and Pamela Taylor. I keep coming back to Pamela Taylor, the former director of a government nonprofit in West Virginia, whose social media response to the presidential election was just about the purest expression of gratuitous white racism I've ever encountered. "It will be so refreshing to have a classy, beautiful, dignified First Lady back in the White House," Ms. Taylor tweeted. "I'm tired of seeing an Ape in heels."

When you consider that Michelle Obama is this brilliant, educated woman who has never harmed Taylor personally and who is superior to her in every conceivable way, Taylor's outburst takes its place as a classic specimen of blind racial hatred. Taylor lost her job, of course, but when did she lose her soul? When she dies, they should send her brain to researchers who study the pathology of racism, to see if there was some particular neural train wreck that made Pamela Taylor what she was.

"No matter how much money you have, no matter how famous you are, no matter how many people admire you, being black in America is tough," the activist NBA superstar LeBron James reflected, after thugs spray-painted racial slurs on his $21 million home in Los Angeles. After the election in November, James endorsed the safety-pin movement, which urged white people who had not voted for Donald Trump to wear a safety pin on their clothing, a sign to non-white Americans that they were "safe." "Do it," James recommended last fall, "because I just don't have the time or energy to hate you all." I wore one on my lapel a couple of times, until I realized that no one recognized the gesture, and just assumed that I was another eccentric old white man. How do we communicate trust, how do we let each other know that we're not boiling with pointless hatred? That's the sorry state of America in 2017.

Blueprint for Sorrow

THE SINGULAR CAREER OF
W. SIDNEY PITTMAN, ARCHITECT

2015

U nfairly but inevitably, the cultural history of the South has been divided into two distinct epochs, one before and the other after "The
Sahara of the Bozart," the merciless carpet-bombing of all things
Southern that H. L. Mencken published in the *New York Evening Mail* in
1917. Mencken was typically disinclined to buttress his prejudices with
strenuous research or reporting, but at that moment he was by far the most
influential and quotable critic in America. His sweeping indictment was delivered in language so ringing and memorable that the scars left by his scorn
can still be seen today. Proud Southerners had no dignified recourse when
the great man compared their artistic accomplishments to the best of Serbia
or Albania. After such a blanket disparagement, it would have been pathetic
for them to point lamely to an adequate pianist in Savannah, a promising
painter in Birmingham, a Richmond poet who seemed better than average.
After the initial spasms of indignation, the South could only shut its mouth,
open its eyes, and try to do better.

Which it did, of course, as even Mencken conceded a few years later,
though he twisted the blade again by claiming all the credit for the "Rena-
scence" of the humiliated Southland. It's ironic that white Southerners were
so stung by his contempt for their culture, yet troubled so little by his contempt for their racial arrangements—which in 1917, not long after the glorification of the Ku Klux Klan by D. W. Griffith in *Birth of a Nation* (1915),
could scarcely have been uglier or more indecent. Mencken probably
intended his litany of the South's intellectual and creative deficiencies as
mere prologue to harsher invective, occurring a few paragraphs later: "The
most booming sort of piety, in the South, is not incompatible with the
theory that lynching is a benign institution. Two generations ago, it was not
incompatible with an ardent belief in slavery."

A few critics must have noted that "The Sahara" is a close echo, if not an adaptation, of a critical essay published in 1820 in the *Edinburgh Review* by the English cleric Sydney Smith, the most celebrated wit of his day. Smith's target was the entire United States of America. After a lengthy catalog of American inadequacies—"In the four quarters of the globe, who reads an American book? Or goes to an American play? Or looks at an American picture or statue?" ("Who drinks out of American glasses? . . . or sleeps in American blankets?)—he concludes his jeremiad in language even stronger than Mencken's: "Finally, under which of the old tyrannical governments of Europe is every sixth man a slave, whom his fellow creatures may buy and sell and torture?"

There's no question that Sydney Smith's extended sneer had come to Mencken's attention; he quotes it in the first chapter of the first edition of *The American Language*, his eccentric, irreplaceable masterwork on North American English published in 1919. Smith and Mencken, separated by a century, were both urbane rationalists appalled by slavery and racist theory. Smith seems to have despised Americans as thoroughly as Mencken, a native of Baltimore, despised the citizens of deeper Dixie. But only Mencken published a racial theory of his own to explain the intellectual wasteland, the immense cultural vacuum he saw stretching "south of the Potomac." Mencken postulated that the vanishing Southern aristocracy, the old planter class that contributed so many of the Founding Fathers, had never stooped to breed with white trash. All its blue-chip DNA, he theorized, had been inherited by the children of African slaves and mixed-race mistresses, who were now the South's genetic aristocracy—its true talent, however suppressed— while the simian white rabble dragged its knuckles and drowned in a stagnant gene pool.

As far as I know, no one ever tried to assassinate Henry Mencken. That he could offer such an incendiary theory even half-seriously, in the heyday of the Klan, gives us a rough idea of his reckless courage. At the same time, of course, he was opposing American intervention in World War I and all but publicly rooting for the kaiser. Today, when pundits no less than politicians pander shamelessly to the mobs and wear team colors—or pretend to inhabit nonexistent middle ground—Mencken's impudent independence takes our breath away. But he may have overlooked at least one remarkable example of his radical racial theory at work. Among the many cultural ornaments the South lacked, according to "The Sahara of the Bozart," were architects ("not even a bad one between the Potomac mud flats and the Gulf") and "a single public monument that is worth looking at."

If he had been aware of the singular history of W. Sidney Pittman, architect, he might have softened those assessments. There's no record that Mencken ever visited the Jamestown Tercentennial Exposition of 1907, a world's fair commemorating three centuries of Anglophone settlement in North America. President Theodore Roosevelt and the aging literary eminence Mark Twain both attended—twice each—along with Standard Oil tycoon Henry Rogers and rafts of senators, congressmen, and foreign diplomats. Though the exposition fell short of attendance projections and bankrupted its organizers, one of its most innovative and successful features was the Negro Building, an unprecedented tribute to the cultural achievements of Black Americans. The building's exhibits and architecture were critically acclaimed and drew 750,000 visitors, most of them white men. (It was, of course, the only building non-whites were allowed to enter.) Roosevelt praised it and toured it on both his visits to Jamestown.

The Negro Building was planned, funded, designed, constructed, and staffed by African Americans only. Its architect was thirty-two-year-old William Sidney Pittman, a graduate of Tuskegee Institute in Alabama and Drexel Institute (now University) in Philadelphia. His commission for the Negro Building was the first U.S. government contract ever awarded to an African American architect. The year 1907 was a banner year for Pittman. The success of his building preceded his marriage in October to the daughter of Booker T. Washington, legendary president of Tuskegee—another distinguished visitor to the Jamestown Exposition, though Dr. Washington was the only celebrity whose tour was limited to one pavilion.

A brief four decades after emancipation, very few young Black men in the United States could have viewed their lives with as much optimism as Sidney Pittman in 1907. Professional success and the new commissions that came with it, international recognition, an attractive wife who was a classically trained pianist and whose father was the most influential and widely admired African American alive—Pittman at thirty-two was the lucky one man in a million, and no doubt the focus of considerable envy. Not all Black Americans viewed the Negro Building, with its crafts displays and historical dioramas, as a source of pride and hope. W. E. B. Du Bois and journalist Timothy Thomas Fortune, leading the first wave of African Americans who could legitimately be called civil rights activists, denounced the segregated

exposition and its Negro Building as a typically Southern, condescending "Jim Crow affair" that demeaned the Black experience. The pragmatic,
accommodating "first education, then equality" philosophy of Booker T.
Washington was anathema to the Du Bois faction. (H. L. Mencken, no
doubt preoccupied with his book on Friedrich Nietzsche that was published
in 1908, is not known to have weighed in on the Jamestown controversy.)

Black radicals, then as now, were a small, beleaguered group. Their criticism
was no impediment to Pittman's flourishing career. In the decade following
the exposition, he distinguished himself designing schools, churches, and
other public buildings in and around Washington, DC, including several
college projects and the capital's Black YMCA. In a newspaper profile written in 1910, he was described as "the leading architect of his race." (At this
time, according to one source, no more than fifty Black architects were
practicing in America.) But Sidney Pittman was not a man to rest comfortably on his good fortune and accomplishments. His mentor, Dr. Washington, allowed that he was "a curious and troublesome individual." Always described as exacting and temperamental, he grew restless in the long shadow
cast by his formidable father-in-law. In 1913 he moved his family to Dallas,
where he planted another historical milestone as the first Black architect
to practice in the state of Texas. One of his first commissions was the Colored Knights of Pythias Temple on Elm Street, which for decades served as
a Black community center for the Deep Ellum neighborhood in east Dallas.
When it was designated as an historic landmark in 1989, a nostalgic pres-
ervationist described Pittman's Temple, a handsome four-story Beaux Arts
structure featuring a top-floor ballroom and the only unsegregated elevator
in Dallas, as "the crown jewel of the district."

In those first years he was in considerable demand, designing churches
and libraries in Fort Worth, Waxahachie, and even distant Houston and
San Antonio. But it was in the Lone Star State that an inspiring American success story began to unravel. In the darkest days of Jim Crow, when
pigmentation was fate, the most frustrating curse of color was to be light
enough to pass for white, bright and gifted enough to surpass most whites,
yet still consigned to an inferior class that was never honestly allowed to
compete. Some of these mixed-race unfortunates accepted it with amazing
equanimity, some schemed and struggled and won small battles—and
some raged visibly all their lives. W. Sidney Pittman belonged to the third
group, one that includes some of America's most tragic figures, including
the illustrious W. E. B. Du Bois. "The guy looked as white as any white

man," according to a Dallas historian, Donald Payton. "He suffered the
plight fair-skinned blacks have always suffered. He was too white to be accepted by blacks and too black to be accepted by whites."

He never suffered passively. It was hardly surprising that very few white
citizens had the courage to hire Pittman; what infuriated him was that affluent Blacks who could afford his services—rare birds in Deep Ellum—
often took their business to white architects. Increasingly bitter and eccentric, Pittman became a very difficult man. Within a few years he evolved
from his natural position as one of the leaders of the Black community in
Dallas to become, instead, its fiercest critic. Long on talent, energy, and
principle, he seems to have been short on charm and devoid of tact. His
quarrels with the neighbors and diatribes against the Black clergy alienated
nearly everyone who could have helped him. By 1928 his wife Portia, a beloved music teacher in the Dallas public schools, was so demoralized by his
rages and the family's social isolation that she left him and went home to
Tuskegee.

Her desertion only spurred Pittman to higher, more heated levels of bel-
licose engagement. In 1931 he began to publish his own weekly newspaper
("a scandal sheet," a neighbor remembers), a tabloid he named "Brotherhood Eyes" and dedicated to exposing the selfishness and hypocrisy of the
Black establishment—"to clean the Race of crooked leaders," as he put it.
With a true, almost Menckenesque flair for hyperbole and invective, he had
few supporters but many readers. Robert Wilonsky, writing in the *Dallas
Observer* in 2007, compared Pittman's style to Hunter Thompson "filtered
through an alto sax." (For their research on the life of W. Sidney Pittman, I
am much indebted to Wilonsky and to Mary Barrineau, who profiled the
architect in *The Dallas Times Herald* in 1986.)

Pittman's favorite targets were always the preachers, whom he accused
of enriching themselves at the expense of their poor and ignorant parishioners: "What is it about those who profess to be our spiritual leaders that
impels them to think so much of their own welfare and so little of others?"
he asked his readers, in an editorial published in 1936. "Why is there so little
self-denial and such an excess of selfishness among the salaried shepherds
of His sheep?"

In this broadside Pittman went so far as to charge the local pastors with
raising $1,100 to expedite the criminal prosecution of *Brotherhood Eyes* and
its editor, a charge that has the ring of paranoid fantasy. But just a year
later he was convicted of mailing obscene material—his newspaper—and

sentenced to five years in Leavenworth Penitentiary. A postal inspector who testified at his trial described him as "the brainiest and shrewdest Negro whom I have ever met."

Pittman was paroled in 1939, reportedly through the intervention of his ex-wife's connections in Washington. At some uncertain date he reappeared in Dallas. He lived the rest of his life there as a kind of displaced person, lodging in a series of disreputable hotels, a strange figure in a rumpled, dirty coat and tie and long hair. Old-timers would point him out to their grandchildren with warnings about the sins of pride and wrath.

W. Sidney Pittman died "penniless," as they used to say, in 1958, and was buried in an unmarked grave, in a generous neighbor's family plot. It wasn't until 1985, during the campaign to preserve the Pythian Temple as an historic landmark, that the Dallas Historical Society located his grave in the Glen Oaks Cemetery and dignified it with a granite marker. Pittman's epitaph is from a letter he wrote to Booker T. Washington when he was eighteen years old: "I am here for the right thing and not for the wrong."

Many ironies attach themselves to the grim history of Sidney Pittman, pioneer of genius, the product of a warped society that marginalized him, unhinged him, and then virtually eradicated all evidence of his existence. The Negro Building at Jamestown, which so impressed Theodore Roosevelt and his foreign guests, was demolished within a year. The Pythian Temple, that "crown jewel" often threatened by developers and deliberately neglected by its current owners, is still standing, but in a state of dereliction worse than Pittman at his lowest ever reached. Many of his buildings were demolished, but more have simply vanished from the historical record. A recent survey of his career by the Texas State Historical Association strikes this sorrowful note: "The majority of his structures have not been identified, however, and may never be identified because public records are lacking and Pittman's personal records have not been located."

Even his one microbiography, a thirty-four-page dissertation ("The Life and Legacy of W. Sidney Pittman," Linda Komes, 1992) published by the University of Virginia, is out of print and currently unobtainable through Amazon.com. But some lost records that have recently been recovered frame a further irony, and even lend a curious credence to the scandalous, Klan-baiting racial theories of H. L. Mencken. Those records, from interviews with Pittman while he was an inmate at Leavenworth, reveal that the Black butcher and former slave he once believed to be his father, a man who died when he was four, was actually his stepfather. His father was a white Montgomery lawyer—Pittman was a rich white man's bastard son just like his father-in-law Dr. Washington, whose biological father owned a plantation.

Pittman's son Booker, a jazz clarinetist who played with Louis Armstrong and Count Basie and later emigrated to Brazil, confirmed this lineage in a biography published in Portuguese. Since his mother was a light-skinned mixed-race woman, W. Sidney Pittman was blessed or cursed with a great deal more white blood than the current president of the United States. So it goes, as Kurt Vonnegut Jr. always wrote to punctuate the lamentable and unbearable. Is tragedy all about temperament, or much about timing, too?

PART TWO

Stations of the Cross

Bible Belt Blues

2013

They call it the global village. Nothing goes unobserved, nothing is without distant consequences. A man throws a rock in Pretoria, another man ducks in Helsinki. The world's all wired, or wireless—I have no idea how any of it works, mechanically. This willful ignorance is appalling, even in an English major of Medicare age, but it's grounded in an invincible lack of interest. Call our technophobia "innovation fatigue." You may find it's chronic in my generation. Though we can't fathom microchips, we don't pretend we're not stunned by their impact. Luxor, Egypt, in January: Drifting along the West Bank of the Nile at sunset in a tall-masted felucca, part of a scene as ancient as the pharaohs, I realized that a sudden dead calm created long odds against crossing the river in time for dinner, or even breakfast if the current carried us far enough downstream. But at the moment of decision the skipper snapped open his cell phone and summoned a cousin with a motorboat to tow us.

The success of Egypt's current revolution has been credited to the internet and the devices that connect its initiates. Popular movements learn, brainstorm, strategize, and raise money online. Even the implacable bullies who rule China and North Korea have been frustrated by technology that enables a freedom-starved younger generation to conspire without congregating. Still, there's a dark side of the global village, a wrong side of the global tracks. In Gainesville, Florida, a fundamentalist minister with a double-digit IQ burns a Quran, for the amusement of three dozen malnourished peckerwoods who make up his congregation—and in Mazar-i-Sharif, Afghanistan, a mob of Muslim fanatics slaughters twelve United Nations workers to avenge this insult to the Prophet. Pastor Terry Jones of the (ironically named) Dove World Outreach Center had the burning videotaped, of course, and streamed it on the church's website. This tiny spark, launched online, took less than two weeks to become a conflagration halfway around the planet. The day after the massacre at the UN compound, thousands of protesters rioted in Kandahar. Nine more people died and eighty were injured. The final body count from Pastor Terry's stupidity may exceed American military casualties for the month of April.

It's not unfair to say that there are more and deadlier idiots in Kandahar than in Gainesville. But the point is that the global village harbors a million village idiots, and no idiot is an island. Not anymore. Pastor Terry was bewildered by the news that he had triggered religious murders, as bewildered as he might be if he ever reads the whole Quran and discovers that he incinerated twenty-five references to his Lord Jesus Christ, all of them positive and respectful. At the least, Muhammad was an admirer of Jesus and an interpreter of his teachings. Linguistic correspondences between their names and similarities in their legends persuade some scholars of monotheism that Jesus and Mohammed—both elusive historically—are semimythical embodiments of the very same religious tradition, set apart only by a few centuries and the divergent mythologizing of their adherents.

Scholars don't get a lot of pulpit time in the Bible Belt. Though educated Southerners despise it as much as any of the stereotypes that still marginalize our people, the image of the heavy-breathing, possibly randy evangelist serving up hellfire to a congregation of barefoot believers with lint in their hair is one that an industrious Yankee reporter can still substantially corroborate, in most communities in the Dixie heartland—from Gainesville all the way up to Winchester, Virginia, where the recently deceased Joe Bageant, unique redneck radical and author of *Deer Hunting with Jesus*, affectionately chronicled his brother the preacher's adventures as an exorcist of demons. Jimmy Swaggart, Oral Roberts, Jerry Falwell, Jim Bakker, Tammy Faye, and company actually walked these hills and thumped these bibles. They were not fictional characters like Elmer Gantry or comic-page caricatures like Al Capp's Marryin' Sam and Walt Kelly's Deacon Mushrat. The unctuous, nausea-inducing Pat Robertson, who blamed 9-11 and Hurricane Katrina on God's anger at America's unrepentant homosexuals, has devoted his whole life to embarrassing the South far more painfully than Terry Jones and his flaming Quran.

Evangelical religion of an extreme stripe—fire and brimstone, biblical inerrancy—thrives in many far corners of the republic, but the South is its wellspring and its homeland. A county-by-county map of America constructed by Dante Chinni and James Gimpel for their book *Our Patchwork Nation* indicates that nearly all the counties colored brown for "Evangelical Epicenters" are in the traditional South and the border state of Missouri.

Religion has been the South's second greatest embarrassment, after race. Unfortunately they've been closely linked. We can never afford to forget that those were crosses the Ku Klux Klan burned at their rallies and lynchings. And there's no denying that most segregationist Protestants of the Jim Crow generations believed that heaven itself was segregated.

When Rob Bell, the influential pastor of an evangelical Michigan megachurch, suggested in his new book *Love Wins* that it's high time Christians set aside archaic notions of a literal, sulfurous, demon-infested hell, all hell broke loose in the Southern synod. They cling passionately to their inferno, these least and cruelest of our Christian brethren, because there's no way on earth they can take adequate revenge on those of us who disagree with them. Though they claim they love us and hope to save us in spite of ourselves.

Hell is the sturdy keystone of gloomy Calvinism. But not all evangelicals, nor even all Southern Baptists, find spiritual comfort in the damnation of others. If we groan and hang our heads over Pat Robertson and Terry Jones, we might stand up and cheer for Christian splinter sects like the Primitive Baptist Universalists of Southwest Virginia and neighboring Appalachia, who were one hundred years ahead of Rob Bell in banishing the devil from their theology. Known disrespectfully as the "no-hellers" to their Christian neighbors, they practice the beautiful heresy of universalism, which holds that all souls originate with God and all return to Him, without exception. Love wins. Never numerous but tenacious in a theologically hostile environment, these mountain Christians hold services characterized by hugging, laughing, crying, and affirming their belief that "people of all creeds, colors, and nationalities will share heaven with them." The great bluegrass musician Ralph Stanley is a member of one of their congregations.

Could any Christian testament be more appealing or humane? Regrettably, the no-hellers seem to number in the hundreds, fewer even than the snake handlers in their native mountains, while sinner-burning churches of the born-again Right enroll Southerners by the tens of millions. Many more books will be written about the American preference for harsh, punitive religion while the rest of the Western world moves toward liberal theology or none at all. In the South, we lose our way entirely when retro religion mates with reactionary politics—a marriage made in hell that produces Rosemary's Babies like Jim DeMint. What impression would the rightwing T-shirt slogan "Babies, Guns, Jesus" make on poor Jesus, a radical rabbi who is not known to have fathered babies or even to have carried a sword, far less an assault rifle? From the cross to the crosshairs, Lord have mercy on us all. One Nation Under Fire.

Southern fundamentalists have bonded with the Tea Party and politicized their pulpits, ignoring the stern warnings of Thomas Jefferson, a universalist sympathizer who believed that separation of church and state was the one indispensable cornerstone of the democracy he invented. Jefferson had "an undying anxiety of anything that would bring church and state together," his biographer, the eminent religious historian Edwin Gaustad, testified in the famous case of the Alabama courthouse adorned with the Ten Commandments. "He was not against religion. He was against any combination of power with religion."

As Muslims, homosexuals, immigrants, a non-white president, and women's reproductive rights face the righteous wrath of its captive politicians, the Christian Right is morphing rapidly into the American Taliban. And it's morphing in full view of a global village that for the most part wishes—believe it or not—to see the United States in the best possible light. But a Terry Jones never travels to the Middle East, and now, if he's remotely sane, he never will.

Of all things most unique and interesting about the Southern states, hell-fire Christianity is one export we should strive to keep out of the global marketplace and the global conversation. If it's not already too late. Yet there are intriguing hints of a thaw, of a new diversity here in the Old Confederacy where even Episcopalians are suspected of subversive doctrines. In Panama City, Florida, roughly two hundred miles from the pyre of the Quran in Gainesville, a popular English teacher named Michael Creamer has organized a successful atheist club as a counterpoint to Christian groups at Rutherford High School. Its membership has doubled this year, though it still falls short of two dozen. In an article in *The New York Times*, reporter Michael Winerip refers to Panama City as the buckle of the Bible Belt (there are many claims to bucklehood) and marvels at the student atheists' easy relationship with other students whose lives are dominated by church and the Junior ROTC.

Will the Bible Belt gradually unbuckle? In my home state of North Carolina, at Fort Bragg of all places, a thriving atheist group that calls itself MASH (Military Atheists and Secular Humanists) is raising money for a concert billed as "Rock Beyond Belief," featuring a prominent rock band and a speech by the British biologist and atheist author Richard Dawkins.

MASH claims that nearly 20 percent of Fort Bragg's soldiers are nonbelievers. When soldiers in North Carolina bill themselves as secular humanists,
we begin to suspect that Jesse Helms is actually dead—back in his heyday
"secular humanist" was right-wing code for "Jew." Another atheist group,
the Triangle Freethought Society, is sponsoring an "Out of the Closet" series of billboards in Raleigh, featuring the photographs and testimony of
ordinary citizens who don't believe in God. A UNC professor of religion,
Bart Ehrman, writes books explaining that the Bible is a deceptive literary
grab bag authored by just about everyone except God. Though Dr. Ehrman
is constantly reviled in Letters to the Editor, so far no one has tried to lynch
him.

These are rays of light in a state where the constitution specifically pro-
hibits nonbelievers from holding public office. The increasing visibility
of religious skeptics encourages me, as a fellow traveler. But I guess I betray my age when I shy away from the word "atheist." It was used as a slur,
with nearly the sting of "queer" or "commy," when it was directed against
my father's family of Universalists fifty years ago. "Atheist?" I probably replied. "No, no, look, there's our church with the stained-glass windows and
the carved pulpit, there's the big organ where my grandmother plays the
hymns. We're Christians just like you."

Not just like you, exactly, because Unitarian Universalists revere Christ
but deny his divinity—like Muslims. And my grandparents' fancy church
was one of a kind among freethinkers, built with the generous participa-
tion of a billionaire parishioner, the railroad baron George Pullman. I don't
mean to claim that Universalists faced active discrimination as Muslims
or Hindus might have—this congregation was distinctly middle class—but
there was an understanding that even the children of Universalists should
avoid theology in casual conversation. On the other hand, we were led to
understand that George Washington, Thomas Jefferson, Benjamin Franklin, John Adams, and Abraham Lincoln were our soul brothers, even if
they never joined the church, and reminded that the membership included
John Quincy Adams, Millard Fillmore, William Howard Taft, and Adlai
Stevenson. This distinguished liberal family might be a prideful stretch in
some ways, but a simple truth the Christian Right deplores is that America
was not founded or defined by Holy Rollers.

Universalism is still dear to me; I think it's inspiring that Enlightenment
intellectuals and unlettered Appalachian Baptists arrived at the same sweet
doctrine from entirely different traditions and assumptions. Early on, I

moved beyond the church's teachings and decided that the creator of the universe, if such an entity existed, was unlikely to resemble human beings in any way. If by some quirk (he/she) did, however, it would certainly be the rarer, finer part of the human package the creator would reflect—mercy, forgiveness—and not the nasty piece that includes violence, sadism, and revenge. That settled it for hell, of course, and also for the vain bully who passes for God in the Old Testament. I used to say, whistling past the gates of hell, that I had no interest in any god who seemed meaner and dumber than I was. Or weirder. Read Leviticus for a mind-bending crash course in the obsessive-compulsive personality.

"Atheist" is a title I never coveted. The bestselling atheist authors like Dawkins and Christopher Hitchens seem immodestly confrontational to me, and the God they reject, the alpha male Yahweh with a lot of attitude and a lot of rules, is an easy target unworthy of their intellects. The grumpy god who rewards or punishes is a children's god, designed, like the devil, to make simple people behave. More challenging definitions of God have enriched the theological conversation for a long, long time. Back in the seventeenth century, the Jewish philosopher Baruch Spinoza, sitting grinding lenses in his shop in The Hague, conceived of a God inseparable from nature, from creation—"God is the world" sums up Avishai Margalit's interpretation of Spinoza's deity.

Contemporaries described the ascetic genius Spinoza as a "God-intoxicated man," and his God encompassed everything that humbled humanity and stretched the limits of its understanding and imagination. Though "agnostic" is a label that concedes human ignorance in a modest way I respect, I'd rather be called a "pantheist," a Spinozan like Emerson, like Einstein. "God is the awareness of the infinite in each of us," Annie Dillard wrote once, and that simple formula works for me. I may be ignorant and skeptical, but I'm not insensible, not incurious, not emptied of spiritual potential.

In a nutshell—not a hard shell—that's how it looks to me now, with final things not so far ahead as they used to be. What's the difference between my testimony and the preaching of Pat Robertson or even Billy Graham? For one thing, there's not a missionary bone in my body. If everyone who read this suddenly decided that I was 100 percent right, I'd begin to lose confidence that I was on the right track. The biggest problem with organized religions, especially with fundamentalist religions from Gainesville to Kandahar, is that they require and compel consensus. The important part of religion is what you believe when you're in your room alone, not what you profess to believe in a crowd of believers. Alone in that room, your remote corner of the all-wired global village, you can send out a spiritual message in search of a soulmate. Or, to be on the safe side, you can even keep it to yourself. As I know I'll manage to do, someday soon.

Godforsaken

OF DEATH AND DAFFODILS

2020

Here in North Carolina, it was the kind of April day that inspires poets, with a rainwashed blue sky and everything in bloom — dogwood, azalea, redbud, wisteria, and a dozen varieties of tiny anonymous flowers pushing up through the deep grass in my lawn. If you haven't lived in the Carolinas, you couldn't be expected to understand how beautiful April can be, with the light green of new leaves as backdrop for all that fleeting color.

Actually it was an inauspicious day, historically, the same day John Wilkes Booth shot Abraham Lincoln, the day when RMS *Titanic* struck an iceberg in the North Atlantic and sank in three hours, with a loss of 1,500 lives. April 14, 2020, for all its perfection, was a tragically shadowed day as well. Several weeks into the nationwide quarantine imposed for the corona virus pandemic, we were becoming accustomed to newswire photos of coffins stacked behind nursing homes and forlorn masked figures standing in long lines in the rain, waiting to be tested. On the one hand, new life abundant; on the other hand, its stark and stunning opposite. It reminded me of another spring day a few years ago, and an image I've never been able to delete from my memory banks.

I was walking across the lawn of the Burwell School, a block from my house, when I spied a huge bed of daffodils in perfect bloom. I detoured for a closer look, but when I reached the flowers I could see that they formed a bower for a large gray tomcat, stone dead. He had not been dead long, the poor cat, and retained his physical integrity. The flies and ants and the local flock of black vultures had not yet disturbed his final rest among the daffodils. I left him there. I'm not sure what else I should have done. This was years before I might have been carrying a cell phone with a camera. But the image, that intimate interface between life and death, has never left me.

The impression it made was deeply personal, no doubt. In the second bewildering month of a national nightmare, my indelible vision of death among the daffodils offered no obvious lesson for surviving social distancing and viral paranoia. Except perhaps, for those fortunate enough to own yards, the suggestion that you're better off watching things grow in your yard than watching things die on your television. But the South's gorgeous Silent Spring of 2020 begged to be experienced as a constant irony, the same irony T. S. Eliot is working in "The Waste Land" when he writes, "April is the cruelest month, breeding / Lilacs out of the dead land." I'll wager that April's cruelty has been invoked repeatedly this year, by nearly every journalist who ever passed freshman English.

Yet cruel it remained, a daily experience of life and death almost inseparable, an unavoidable collision of incompatible emotions. How we dealt with it spoke volumes about who we were, at the deepest levels. I appreciated the friends who obsessively circulated graveyard humor about the pandemic, efforts to cheer me up that were largely futile. I was less tolerant of the ones who tried to make light of it, as if quarantine and social isolation were really a minor inconvenience, even a rare opportunity to finish a novel or plant a new garden. There's a certain flavor of oblivious optimism that infuriates me. But the contrast in plague response that told me the most about myself originated with an article in *The New York Times*, an interview with a young woman who teaches at Duke University, where years ago I also taught a couple of courses.

Kate Bowler, a religious historian who was diagnosed with incurable cancer when she was thirty-five, carries an authority I can't approach when it comes to mortality. I liked the title of the book she wrote about her experience with illness and fear—*Everything Happens for a Reason: And Other Lies I've Loved*—and I was impressed by most of her answers to the reporter's questions, especially her dismissal of the American mandate to "stay positive" through the worst of times. "It adds shame to suffering," she said, for everyone who fails to see the silver lining. Excellent, I thought. "A pandemic is not a judgment," she added, "and it will not discriminate between the deserving and the undeserving."

I was on board with Dr. Bowler all the way until I reached this statement: "I think moments like this reveal to me God's unbelievable love for us." Tough love, my inner Nietzsche responded with a sneer, and I remembered that she teaches at Duke Divinity School. I am not on the same page with a theo-

logian who finds evidence of love—or hate, or any sort of divine intention—
in a viral pandemic.

Can't we just leave God out of this, for once? Theodicy—the vindication of God, roughly speaking, the belief that all history's agonies and blessings are a part of God's plan—is the conundrum that probably kept me
from attending divinity school, which was briefly a part of my plan. One of
the most amiable purveyors of popular religion is the syndicated columnist
Rabbi Marc Gellman, whose "God Squad" reflections are consistently sane
and humane. But Rabbi Gellman is a hardcore theodician, and his column
on the pandemic, well written and deeply felt, merely expanded the rhetorical gulf that separates me from God's loyal defenders.

"Even the coronavirus is not evil," Gellman wrote. "It is just a part of
God's plan for the governance of the world." And even more sanguine, in
the same vein, "The coronavirus may be a warning from God to help each
other."

At this point I'm shaking my head, even grinding my teeth. Must God
always get a free pass? I never believed in a god whose deliberations, intentions, or actions were even remotely comprehensible to human beings,
and I think it's obvious that the god of rewards and punishments was
invented by ancient priests and theocrats to keep our unruly race in order.
Yet the rationalization required for the popular belief in a fully omnipotent,
eternally benevolent deity has always mystified and fascinated me. The
logic of denial is all too clear. The British philosopher Richard Swinburne,
one of God's most eloquent modern apologists, writes "Without a theodicy,
evil counts against the existence of God."

Exactly. But if this god is omnipotent, fully capable of answering desperate prayers and deflecting catastrophes like this pandemic, then is he not, in
any human terms, unjust and morally compromised? And if he's innocent
because he's helpless or limited in his power, then of course he's not God
with a capital letter as every monotheistic religion presents him. Logically
there's no middle road that doesn't involve intricate, unconvincing theological gymnastics. God, in relation to human suffering, is either cruel or irrelevant. And irrelevant is equivalent to absent.

It's not my intention to play Richard Dawkins, deflating orthodox religious faith just when some people may need it most. The other factor in
these theological equations is the word "evil," invariably employed to mean
"harmful and destructive to human beings." But that's a very limited, an-

thropocentric definition of evil. Let's agree that "God" is the creator and protector of the planet Earth and all the life it sustains, as most religions maintain. If that's true, and the human race is, as most scientists would concede, the most violent, destructive, and overwhelming life form ever to dominate the earth—a kind of viral pandemic ourselves—then it's possible to reimagine the coronavirus as one of the tools God has chosen to defend his creation.

What if *Homo sapiens* is not God's cherished work in progress, as the Bible and the theologians would have it, but a terrible mistake He recognizes and is scrambling to correct? It's an unpleasant thought, but hardly an irrational one. If it's necessary to believe in an engaged, hands-on God, a Green God striving to defuse the human population bomb is more appealing than a careless God dispensing pardons to his left and death sentences to his right, like the dealer in some deadly game of cards.

I've never been convinced that God is either with us or against us. If I'm in need of metaphysical counsel, I tend to turn not to Richard Swinburne but to an earlier British philosopher, the formidable skeptic Bertrand Russell. Russell, whose sixty-odd published works include *Why I Am Not a Christian*, turned up his nose at debates over God's true intentions or the eternal struggle between good and evil. Asked whether he found the universe benevolent or malignant, he suggested that it was cosmically indifferent, at least to the fate of humanity.

The controversy that always surrounded Russell, a self-described pacifist, socialist, and agnostic, hasn't hurt his enduring reputation as one of the wisest men of the twentieth century. The internet, which Russell (1872–1970) mercifully never lived to see, is spiced with so many selections and quotations from the philosopher's work that you can move from link to link and spend several days without exhausting your curiosity. No one who makes the effort has ever regretted it. Russell's contemporary Virginia Woolf once wrote of him in her diary, envyingly, "I should like the run of his headpiece." Fifty years after his death, any glimpse into that prized headpiece remains rewarding, not just because Russell writes so well—he won a Nobel Prize for Literature in 1950—but because, in a world of multiplying absurdities, he relentlessly makes sense.

And it's not inappropriate—unless you're seeking comfort—to turn to the great Victorian dissenter in times of grief and disaster like the 2020 pandemic. In spite of the advantages of wealth and aristocracy, his long life was marked by a host of sorrows, beginning with the deaths of his parents and his sister when he was a small child. The orphaned genius survived Hitler, Stalin, the Spanish flu pandemic, two monstrous world wars, and the bombing and near conquest of Britain; he served six months in Brixton Prison for his opposition to World War I. He had a miserable first marriage and many domestic upheavals, and his only son was schizophrenic.

He wrote in his autobiography that he was a severely depressed teenager, considering suicide until he was rescued by a passion for mathematics. "The secret of happiness," Russell wrote in what must have been a dark moment, "is to face the fact that the world is horrible, horrible, horrible." He meant the human world, of course, not the natural world that humans have so recklessly exploited. Through it all he refused to accept the comforts of religion, which he had rejected in his adolescence. What he prescribed instead was disarmingly simple: Courage.

"There is something feeble, and a little contemptible, about a man who cannot face the perils of life without the help of comfortable myths," Russell wrote. And on another occasion added, "If we must die, let us die sober, not drunk with pleasant lies."

It's one thing to embrace Russell's stoicism intellectually, quite another to face the imminent possibility of your own death with philosophical calm. In the age of science, individuals still capable of imagining the Lord as their kindly shepherd, as in the 23rd Psalm, are no doubt the lucky ones. For the rest of us, the Valley of the Shadow of Death is a lonely hike. In April 2020 the Valley lay before us, disguised by the splendor of spring.

"Stiff upper lip," the ancient code of Britain's military aristocracy, may seem like a simplistic response to such a calamity. And "Man up!" is sexist. But it was nearly a century ago that Russell wrote *Why I Am Not a Christian*, dismantling twenty centuries of Christian theology with all the merciless logic at his command. Like the fierce skeptic and agnostic H. L. Mencken, who thought his mocking dispatches from the Scopes "Monkey" Trial in 1925 had fatally wounded America's fundamentalists, Bertrand Russell would be appalled to find that primitive creationists and Bible literalists still thrive in the USA. And further discouraged to find an essay headlined "The Pandemic and the Will of God" in an April 2020 edition of *The New York Times*.

Unlike most "conservative" religious commentary, the essay by the Catholic conservative Ross Douthat is neither smugly condescending nor hypocritical. But Douthat can't free himself from the old curse of theodicy. "The purpose of suffering may be mysterious, but we must search for meaning," he writes. His believer's purpose is to explore the possible "meanings" of what is essentially an unfortunate clash between two biological entities, a clash no more momentous, cosmically, than when a snake swallows a frog or a weed poisons a cow. He has forfeited every agnostic reader when he concludes—eloquently—"that meaningless suffering is the goal of the devil, and bringing meaning out of suffering is the saving work of God."

I don't begrudge anyone his "faith," that word, that concept despised by both Russell and Mencken. But faiths beset with gods and devils make frightened children of us all. The Judeo-Christian metaphors of father and son, lord and servant, shepherd and sheep no longer satisfy the transcendental requirements of most educated adults, and the religion they support has been losing ground rapidly in every developed nation. Except of course the United States. The least convincing metaphor in Christianity's repertoire is teacher and pupil, the idea that each disaster is divine pedagogy in disguise. If the coronavirus kills you, it's a random misfortune, not a divine judgment or a lesson from on high for your survivors. If it spares you, it's no confirmation of God's love or mercy or special favor. If it bankrupts you or locks you down until your mind snaps, that's not a test of your faith.

That gray cat in the daffodils was not singled out for his wickedness; the month of April with its deceitful beauty was not chosen to torment the afflicted. Russell would insist that there is no "meaning" in our suffering except what we're able to extract on our own, through hard study, once we've freed ourselves from fear and tired dogma. He believed that there's no dignity in our deaths unless we meet them with confidence in our own perceptions and judgments, our own private awareness of the infinite. It's true that he was guilty of the sin of intellectual pride.

Christian Soldiers

2017

> Under a government which imprisons any unjustly, the true
> place for a just man is also a prison ... the only house in
> a slave state in which a free man can abide with honor.
> —HENRY DAVID THOREAU, "Civil Disobedience"

The death of Daniel Berrigan, a personal hero and one of the few men alive who was old enough to be my father, called up disturbing memories of another critical period in American history. One memory in particular. I was a fledgling journalist at *Time* magazine in New York, newly wed and freshly radicalized by the terrible events of 1968, when Robert Kennedy and Martin Luther King were assassinated, Richard Nixon was elected president, and a misbegotten war in Vietnam divided this country as it has never been divided since—until, perhaps, at this moment. One of my colleagues was dating a tall, pretty young woman named Ann Berrigan. A few of us were drinking at her apartment one late-winter night in 1969. A guest looking for the bathroom started to open a door in the hall—and Ann jumped up almost screaming to warn him, "Don't open that door—don't!" Everyone was startled, and mystified when she made no effort to explain. After her outburst, the evening ended on a note of embarrassment. Back in the street waiting for a cab, Ann's boyfriend entrusted me with the story. Behind the bedroom door that night was her uncle, the Reverend Daniel Berrigan, SJ, a federal fugitive, a radical priest on the FBI's most-wanted list for his part in the incineration (with homemade napalm) of Selective Service records in Catonsville, Maryland, the previous May. Ann wasn't just protecting her uncle, he explained, but her guests as well. Anyone who actually saw Father Berrigan or could confirm his presence was legally obligated to call the FBI or, like Ann, risk felony prosecution for harboring a fugitive.

I had covered the occupation of Columbia University buildings by Students for a Democratic Society (SDS), interviewed Mark Rudd, and witnessed policemen with billy clubs assaulting tenured professors. In New York I'd undergone a rapid evolution from Rockefeller Republican to pacifist and Berrigan fellow traveler, all while the long black shadow of the draft board still lay across my future like a napalmed corpse. But Dan Berrigan hiding just down the hall, on the other side of a thin apartment wall—this was closer to the heart of civil disobedience and radical royalty than I had ever imagined I would be. Later I heard Ann talk about her Uncle Dan and Uncle Phil—Dan's younger brother, a Josephite priest and a war hero—with pride in their exploits but anxious comprehension of the dangers to which these fugitives of conscience had exposed their friends and family. Every good Catholic family is proud of its priests, but the Berrigans had produced a fearless pair of militants the conservative Catholic hierarchy could never endorse or restrain.

Father Dan was the poet, the intellectual of the brothers Berrigan. His first book of verse, *Time Without Number* had won the prestigious Lamont Poetry Prize in 1957, establishing him at thirty-six as a leading figure among Catholic poets. English poetry was my focus as an undergraduate, and for a draft deferment I had been teaching literature at a New England boarding school. As a federal fugitive, Dan Berrigan represented the confluence of serious poetry and nonviolent resistance to the government of the United States—to me, at that time, an irresistible combination. I read most of Berrigan's work that was then in print. Impressed by his craftsmanship and passion, I was an unlikely candidate for his brotherhood of faith. His poem "The Face of Christ" begins "The tragic beauty of the face of Christ shines in our faces." A pilgrim like me, from a family of agnostics, Unitarians, and hardheaded, freethinking Scots, is not instantly engaged. But what fascinated and haunted me was the life where his intellect and faith had led him, a life that in a few months would place him in a prison with felons who may never have read a poem.

The Berrigan brothers' crusade against the Vietnam War and imperial America was one of the first unqualified examples of "high seriousness" I encountered, outside of a book. What they were attempting opened a wider avenue of dissent for so many of us, still politically unformed, who were trying to refine and respond to our consciences. The "higher power" inspiring Dan and Phil Berrigan was so transparently, mountainously higher than the power represented by Nixon and Agnew (and the amoral, Machiavellian Kissinger) that it shamed a whole generation out of the adolescent patriotism we were raised on. Atheists or evangelicals, boys who followed the Berrigans' example and burned their draft cards understood—in a way most of their fathers never had—that defying cynical politicians and bad laws was not the same as betraying your country. And that betraying your conscience was the worst crime of all.

Raised like the Berrigans in a rural, predominantly Catholic community in upstate New York, I grew up with a weakness for priests. Maybe it was their celibacy, freely giving up the one thing I desired most, that intrigued me. But I always knew one or two, and I used to play golf in the early morning, on the dew-drenched fairways most duffers avoid, with an Irish priest who cheerfully tried to convert me to some respectable form of Christianity. I called him "Father" though he asked me to call him "Tom." He looked like Nick Nolte and died young, of cancer. From my secular viewpoint, priests carried an otherness about them that Protestant clergymen did not share. Most of them assigned to our rural parish came from exotic places like Manhattan, Buffalo, Albany. The nearest university, attracting the best Catholic students from my school, was St. Bonaventure, where Thomas Merton had once taught English literature among the brown-robed Franciscans I regarded with exaggerated curiosity and respect.

Dan Berrigan revered Merton, author of the religious classic *The Seven Storey Mountain*, and always claimed him as an intellectual and spiritual father. I met Father Dan only once, many years after his imprisonment and rehabilitation, at a funeral attended by luminaries of the Left. I told him about the night at his niece's apartment, which he found amusing as ancient history. I didn't get a fair chance to sample his famous dry wit. It was his brother Philip with whom I made significant acquaintance, and from whom I received a late education in pacifism, commitment, and Christian sacrifice—a brief but not superficial glimpse of the singular mind of an individual who could live as the Berrigans lived.

In the eternal struggle between the flesh and the spirit, it was the weakness that I always understood. Phil Berrigan, as much as anyone I ever met, showed me the strength. In May of 1994 he and two of his pacifist commandos were locked in the county jail in Edenton, North Carolina, awaiting trial for applying their hammers of justice to the nose cones of F-15E fighter planes at Seymour Johnson Air Force Base. Phil, then seventy, had already spent more years in prison than Mohandas Gandhi. A former semi-pro ballplayer and an infantry lieutenant at the Battle of the Bulge, he was still physically imposing—to carry out his symbolic assault on the F-15Es he climbed an eight-foot fence, forded a freezing knee-deep stream, and crossed three-quarters of a mile of pavement on his hands and knees.

A tough cookie, this warrior priest, who talked about his eleven-plus years in prisons the way scholars talk about graduate school. Sympathetic to his cause, I hadn't known what to expect from him or his fellow prisoners of conscience. I'm profoundly claustrophobic, and people who would give up their physical freedom for their beliefs, for any beliefs, stood well outside my experience. Maybe I anticipated some kind of feverish, hollow-eyed fanatics. What Berrigan showed me instead was the supernatural self-control, the peace and apparently impregnable calm that must come with a firm belief in a benevolent personal God. If I try to describe myself at that time—as my forties ended—"disillusioned" and "skeptical" are words that come to mind. I had not found a God like Berrigan's, and doubted that I ever would—but only an idiot would have failed to recognize the power that it gave him. One of the things I remember best about this strange encounter in the Chowan County jail is that the deputies and jailers—none of them educated or Catholic, I would guess—seemed almost as impressed with their prisoners as I was. They were respectful, almost gentle with Phil Berrigan and big John Dear, a Duke-educated Jesuit, and their younger disciple, Bruce Friedrich.

At least in my presence they were gentle, and it's not as if I was Mike Wallace and the crew from *60 Minutes*. A mild irony was that Philip Berrigan, for all his sacrifice and the transfiguring power of his faith, was not immune to the call of the flesh. He secretly married a former nun in 1970, when he was still a working priest, and later fathered three children. This was a weakness he shared with the great Thomas Merton. Merton (not unlike Saint Augustine) earned a reputation as a libertine in his student days at Cambridge, and was forever susceptible to wine, women, and song—jazz, in the latter case. The Kentucky writer James Still, a friend of mine, used to sneak six-packs of beer into the Abbey of Gethsemani to share with this imperfect monk, whose (avowedly) platonic love affair with a student nurse in Louisville caused a scandal at the Abbey when Merton was fifty and world-famous.

Dan Berrigan seems to have been the true ascetic, the one best suited for the priesthood or the monastery. For most of his ninety-five years he owned virtually nothing, and according to the people who loved him he never noticed the absence of material things that most Americans take for granted.

This was an ideal condition to which I always aspired—of all the monastic vows, poverty would have been the easiest for me—but never quite managed to achieve. (Chastity, silence, obedience—are you serious?) In a diseased consumer culture like America's, uncontaminated citizens like Daniel Berrigan have been viewed as exotic aliens. Of all the quotes I've collected from compatriots whose wisdom was inadequately celebrated, my favorite is a premature self-epitaph from Patrick Hemingway, retired big-game guide and son of the famous Papa: "Say what you will about me, call me an underachiever, but I was never a consumer, and I was never a fan."

I like to think the Berrigans read Hemingway's boast somewhere, and shared it with satisfaction. The strength their neighbors squandered getting and spending, these brothers devoted to emulating Jesus, as they understood him, and pleasing God. I thought a lot about their faith, after witnessing it in practice in the Chowan County jail. The essential work of their lives was conscience building—deciding (or learning, the scholarly Jesuit might have said) exactly what God expects of your conscience and obeying, without question, as long as you live. The voice of your conscience becomes the same as the voice of your god. A god I approved of, in their case, even if I couldn't share him. Theirs was no soft, malleable, spongy sort of god who forgives us for everything, or who can be molded to any desperate purpose—the worst examples of this all-too-human heresy would be the KKK using the cross of Dan Berrigan's Jesus as a symbol of racist terrorism, or jihadists murdering other Muslims (and others) in the name of a homicidal god. The Berrigans' God was a harder god they followed down a hard road; the best consciences I ever witnessed under pressure weren't half as strict as theirs.

Their brand of radical pacifism was too demanding to attract a host of disciples—Jesus barely managed double figures, after all—but the quality of their converts was very high. John Dear, the Jesuit from North Carolina who was jailed in Edenton with Phil Berrigan, has been arrested seventy times for nonviolent protests and served several years in prison. He was dismissed by the Jesuits in 2013 because his passion for peace, in the eyes of his superiors, had compromised his vows of obedience to the order. "Obedience to God comes first," I remember Dear saying, in his jail cell in 1994. But many of us in North Carolina are extremely proud of him for sustaining the work of the Plowshares movement, for keeping the faith as he inherited it from the Berrigans.

Phil Berrigan died in 2002. Now Dan is gone, too, and John Dear, a vigorous young lion of a priest when I met him, is nearing sixty. *The New York Times* describes the peace movement as "withering"; the Pentagon and the Society of Jesus operate much as they did before the Plowshares priests took up their hammers. The secretary of state who supervised America's involvement in the Middle East carnage was narrowly defeated in the 2016 presidential election by a saber-rattling right-wing maniac who raves about bombing Arab countries until the sand glows. After thirteen years, at a cost of over \$2 trillion and 4,500 American deaths, the United States of America—which defeated Hitler, Tojo, and Mussolini in less than four years—has failed to "secure" the single city of Baghdad or the highway to its airport. All of Vietnam's lessons remain stubbornly unlearned.

"This is the worst time of my life," an eighty-seven-year-old Dan Berrigan said in 2008, the last year of the Bush-Cheney-Rumsfeld war machine. "I have never had such meager expectations of the system." But he was in firm command of the irony involved in making great sacrifices for an apparently hopeless cause. He preached that believing in God and doing the right thing, regardless of consequences, were the imperatives that kept a decent person sane. "The day after I'm embalmed," he vowed, "that's when I'll give it up." His refusal to retreat or despair reminded me of the day I spent with his brother Phil in the Edenton jail.

"Is there a temptation to despair and quit, to fold up our tents and go back to normalcy, to our personal requirements?" Phil asked himself, and his comrades. "I suppose. But the consequences of withdrawal are reprehensible. Silence lends assent, doesn't it? Jesus didn't withdraw. I preserve a lot of hope."

"We're prey to discouragement," he admitted when we were alone, the last thing he said to me before the cell door clicked shut on him again. "The public resists the lessons of history—it scarcely acknowledges history. Americans seem tired of perplexing social issues. It comes from the way we live in this country, I guess."

Neither their country nor their church ever lived up to the Berrigans' expectations, and nothing about the way we live in this country offers much hope that there will be another generation of radical priests to hold America's feet to the spiritual fire. There are no schools that breed Christian soldiers of their unbending creed, to insist as they did that war, militarism, and gun violence are all one disease, and one linked inseparably to all the other diseases—oppression, poverty, starvation, racism, environmental degradation—that threaten to bring the human adventure to a premature conclusion. War is insane and disgusting, and it will be with us always, undermining most progress in the direction of civilization. Frustrated pacifists find consolation in the conviction that we're on the right side of history. That consolation is more powerful, apparently, for those convinced that they're on the right side of a righteous God.

Can traditional religion, burdened by its own history, disrespected by science, crowded almost into the shadows by conspicuous consumption and metastasizing technology, still inspire unusual individuals to live heroically, on a consistently higher moral plane? The answer, for anyone familiar with the Berrigan brothers, is a confident "Yes." But there's always my other question, which I'd never be rude enough to pose to a man of faith: If God made and loves us all, why did he make so many of us cruel and stupid?

I've never forgotten a prayer I learned in summer school from the Jesuits of Canisius College in Buffalo, where an Alsatian priest taught me more and better French in two months than several expensive schools had taught me in six years: *"Mere de dieu, priez pour nous, maintenant et a l'heure de notre mort."*

PART THREE

Politics: Ballots, Bullets, Bedrooms

Sex and the
Southern Politician

2010

M ost Americans who are still curious about John Edwards, former U.S. senator and Democratic nominee for vice president of the United States, will have to buy the books published by his wife and his aide Andrew Young, or pick up *GQ* to read the interview with his mistress, who claims the magazine tricked her into testifying half dressed. At the least, they have to troll gossip websites or watch hideous celebrity shows on TV, hosted by the most vapid and repugnant personalities in the low-rent universe. This all requires an unnatural craving for the tarnished legend of John Edwards, fallen star. But here in sleepy Hillsborough, North Carolina, where I'm living out my sunset years in relative peace and quiet, we have only to walk downtown to stay current. Edwards, rumored to be waiting out his divorce in a rental nearby, has been sighted at Walmart and at several local restaurants, and with his characteristic poor judgment has even made a big evening of drinking with the citizens at the Wooden Nickel, which is the happening place here where nothing too conspicuous has happened since the Tories hanged the Regulators in 1771.

A friend of mine was an eyewitness to this recent folly. He fell into bar conversation with the former senator about the misery of ending a marriage, a mutual source of unhappiness. Later in the evening this young man endeavored to extricate the senator from a semihostile crowd that was muttering about calling the police if Edwards planned to drive away with an illegal excess of alcohol in his blood. This is not the way we usually treat strangers in Hillsborough, but some of the customers may have been reading Mrs. Edwards's book. It all ended without incident, thanks perhaps to my friend. But the celebrity who recently scored the lowest approval rating in tabloid history is putting Hillsborough on the map, in a way many of us would like to avoid. He's becoming a tourist attraction. When I see Nancy

Grace or Greta Van Susteren lurking in the Wooden Nickel, I guess I'll know it's time to move on.

It takes a hard heart to rule out all sympathy for this modern Icarus who has fallen so far, this walking testimonial to the negative potential of ambition, lust, egotism, and magical thinking. General embarrassment seems more appropriate than self-righteous anger. The closer you get to one of these human disasters, the less it resembles its reflection in the media mirror. I never sought or claimed any special connection to the ruined man. Our wives have known each other for decades. Coincidentally, a close friend of mine was a ghostwriter for Edwards's original campaign autobiography, *Four Trials*; in this role he made the acquaintance of Andrew Young and is one of the unfortunate few who have seen the fabled sex tape. Even more improbably, the senator and his family have long been loyal patrons of a Japanese restaurant owned by my family—in fact the manager reports that on one evening this spring, John Edwards and his Judas, Andrew Young, occupied the same seat at the sushi bar a couple of hours apart.

For all that, I can hardly say I know him. Since he entered politics we may have had three or four conversations, only one of any length. But when the Rielle Hunter scandal broke in the fall of 2008, I felt that as a neighbor and a journalist who had endorsed his politics, I owed him a fair assessment of his mistakes and misfortunes. A network producer in California happened to read my essay on Edwards, written before many of the most appalling details were public knowledge. As a result an NBC news camera crew ended up in my living room in Hillsborough last winter, and I ended up pontificating uncomfortably on the *Today* show.

As an outspoken critic of tabloid journalism, I was painfully aware of the irony of adding my voice to this particular chorus. But the subject was a near vice president of the USA, not some horny athlete or reality show primate, and I rationalized that my perspective might be more helpful than many others. The pity, of course, is that I'm not heard on national television all that often—believe it or not—and there was no way to exploit this exposure to denounce the National Rifle Association or the rabid lunacy of what used to be the Republican Party. Any word I uttered that was off message, off Edwards, would have ended up on the cutting-room floor. I've seen the future of journalism and the future is all about sex scandals, not much about global warming.

Edwards has been locked in competition with South Carolina's governor, Mark Sanford, for what we here on Tobacco Road like to call the Jeeter

Lester Award for Incautious Coupling. It was Sanford, attempting to cover up a sex holiday, who provided regional wise guys with our favorite new euphemism for extramarital copulation—"walking the Appalachian Trail." "Walking the trail" should have a long life here in the Bible Belt, where every political aspirant will now be scrutinized for loose morals and hormonal imbalance. I still can't believe that Edwards, running for president, actually made the sex tape and failed to destroy it before he left the bedroom. There's no evidence that he was psychotic, or dropping acid. It's a mystery. Yet I'm not convinced that the Carolinas' marquee adulterers are among the nation's most contemptible. It's notable that Edwards and Sanford were both married to unusually intelligent and capable women—a great thing when you're launching a political career, not so great when you divorce them and they write better books than you could write about what a jerk you are.

Americans nurse strange misconceptions about each other's sexuality. We hillbillies and Southerners fantasize New York apartment scenes too weird to watch on video—yet the New Yorker, typified by a *Time* cover story in 1964 ("What sets Southerners apart? Is poverty too prevalent? Is sex too obsessive?"), has always believed that sexual heat rises with the temperature and the humidity, and boils over under live oaks and Spanish moss. Some of our prominent politicians help to perpetuate this stereotype. But when you marvel at Edwards or Sanford, don't forget New York's Eliot Spitzer, Nevada's John Ensign, or closet gay adventurers like Eric Massa of New York, Larry Craig of Idaho, and Jim McGreevey of New Jersey. Reckless lust in high office is a continental, more accurately an intercontinental phenomenon. In Europe, shocked Americans are ridiculed as prigs and naifs. If we can believe the European press, Italian prime minister Silvio Berlusconi and French president Nicolas Sarkozy practically dash around in their undershorts with fists full of condoms, settling like starved honeybees on any flower that spreads its petals. It sounds as if they run great nations like the harems of the ancient East, surrounded by compliant serving girls, eunuchs, and procurers.

We know now that John F. Kennedy had these sultan's morals, too. In his day the press was too incurious about politicians' sex lives, in radical contrast to the drooling, heavy-breathing voyeurism that reigns today. I was cynical enough as a young man. I'm glad I reached the age of indifference before I learned that JFK and Grace Kelly were sex addicts. I'll argue, though, that the South has a more interesting, more multilayered approach to sexual misbehavior than blasé Europeans or see-no-evil Yankees. On the surface, the Bible rules. The seventh commandment. Not far beneath the surface lurks a surprising tolerance, even a certain clandestine pride in the impudent tomcatting of individuals whose eloquence raises them up—primarily politicians and preachers. Sometimes it's hard to tell these persuasive professions apart.

Southerners have a weakness for the Word. Elmer Gantry might have blushed at the sexual transgressions (and hypocrisy) of Jim Bakker and Jimmy Swaggart, who were larger and nastier than life. If a cable TV pulpit or revival tent can hyperstimulate an impressionable sort of Southern woman, calculate the sex appeal of an orator with a far grander congregation, set against a backdrop of the statehouse, the governor's mansion, or the halls of Congress. "Fast lane, fast ladies," shrugged one seasoned political operative. "Power seduces. It's an old, old story."

Many stories, actually, some of the best with a Deep South flavor. "Sex and the Southern Politician," if that book is ever written, will be as long as Boccaccio's Decameron and twice as raunchy. My sources suggest that the project might employ teams of researchers working diligently for decades, like the Oxford English Dictionary. For an epigraph we have a candid confession by Big Jim Folsom, the hard-drinking giant (6'8") who was governor of Alabama from 1947 to 1951 and 1955 to 1959: "Bait the trap with pussy and you'll catch Big Jim every time."

Folsom was hounded by paternity claims; every time an exceptionally large child was born anywhere in Alabama, rumors would fly. Big Jim may strike the keynote, but the State of Louisiana takes the prize, in the opinion of knowledgeable sources. And I'm fortunate to know some prime ones—Ray Strother and Jim Duffy, grizzled veterans of the Louisiana political wars, wily consultants who have steered many a wayward warrior toward high office. For shameless lechery, Duffy doubts that any public servant can match Louisiana governor Edwin Edwards, the incorrigible Cajun charmer who at eighty-three is still serving hard time for stealing. Edwards's many shady ladies were known to insiders as his "Sweeties." He liked to boast of his "sweet tooth" and later made rude confectionery jokes about his second wife, a child bride whose name was Candy. Candy, incidentally, is now a New Orleans realtor who hasn't ruled out rejoining Edwards if he ever leaves prison alive—though she's had a child by another gentleman since they took the governor away.

In his prime Edwards was unapologetic. Duffy recalls an outraged grande dame who disparaged the governor's morals, eliciting this gracious reply (despite his father's Presbyterian surname, Edwards is three-quarters Cajun and fluently bilingual): "Mon cher, I don't smoke and I don't drink, and where I come from two out of three ain't bad." He didn't mention gambling, to which he was hopelessly addicted. When he trounced the KKK potentate David Duke in his last gubernatorial election, Edwards—arguably the wittiest politician the South has produced—quipped that he and Duke had only one thing in common: "We've both been wizards beneath the sheets."

His most famous boast, just before winning one of his record four terms as governor, was "The only way I can lose this election is if I'm caught in bed with a dead girl or a live boy." When Gary Hart lost his chance at the White House over Donna Rice, Edwards, asked to comment, said he'd wait until he'd seen her picture. There will never be another like him. Naturally he started out to be a preacher, for the Church of the Nazarene. If you knew him well, as Duffy and Strother did, you're not so impressed with John Edwards (no relation). "Just one woman?" Even the child out of wedlock would have raised few eyebrows in Louisiana. But they concede that the video was a showstopping innovation. Another candidate for governor of Louisiana was a preacher named Clyde Johnson, who was so exuberant about a tryst with his Sweetie that he vaulted onto her back porch and was caught in midair by a blast from her husband's 12-gauge ("a fine wing shot," in Strother's words) and sent to his last reward in a state of sin. One Baton Rouge politician and his Sweetie were mugged in their motel room by a holdup team that took all their clothes as well as their money and her car. When he couldn't keep his mistress from calling the police, he called his wife and told her not to watch the local newscast because they'd be spreading lies about him—and then called Strother to bring them something to wear home.

Strother's files and memory overflow with these Rabelaisian tales. Edwin Edwards was only the ultimate flowering of a long tradition, which since his heyday has evolved in an uglier direction, toward Republicans who whore around while espousing family values, like the currently hooker-plagued Senator David Vitter, instead of Democrats like Edwards and Earl Long who whored around while espousing nothing but "Laissez les bon temps rouler." (Until recently Vitter faced a primary challenge from porn star Stormy Daniels, who represents a further stage in the evolution of the Louisiana Sweetie.)

It gets hard to read Louisiana history with a straight face. Strother reckons that the ultimate indignity, the gross insult to the honor of the South that would have set Robert E. Lee to weeping and spurring Traveller toward the barn, was committed by a small-time politician in the employ of Governor John McKeithen (1964–1972). A man whose shamelessness, unlike Edwin Edwards's, was unleavened by wit or intellect, he came in hanging his head to tell Strother—assigned to keep him out of trouble—"The governor's pissed with me." Challenged by a frisky secretary to mate with him on top of a Confederate flag spread across the governor's desk, he had complied so vigorously that the glass desktop had broken and cut her buttocks, which required several stitches to repair. The governor never mentioned the broken glass or the bloodshed. "I wondered about that flag being gone," was his only response.

When McKeithen's son Fox—a five-term Louisiana secretary of state—died in a freak accident in 2005, an obituary referred to him as "the last of the red-hot poppas." If this term didn't mean much outside Louisiana, to the home voter it spoke volumes and registered as a term of affectionate admiration. The great big unavoidable irony is that so many of the "red-hot poppas," who took their wedding vows about as seriously as the posted speed limit, were the South's most progressive and useful politicians, the ones who nudged a reluctant Old Confederacy toward the distant light of civilization. These philanderers we've been joking about all ran against the white supremacists and Klansmen, some of them back when that took real courage. Big Jim Folsom was the first Southern governor to speak out forcefully against segregation. Edwin Edwards was one of a handful of Southern congressmen who supported the Voting Rights Act of 1965. The late Charles "Good Time Charlie" Wilson of Texas was a white-hot poppa who gave his girlfriends pet names like Tornado, Snowflake, and Firecracker, but he was a domestic liberal in congress, years ahead of many of his East Texas constituents. Then of course there was Bill Clinton—I'm writing this on Monica Lewinsky's forty-fourth birthday.

He may be a sad case now, but don't pity North Carolina for electing John Edwards. He was the most progressive senator we ever sent to Washington. Don't forget that for most of Edwards's term in the Senate, our other senator was the Neanderthal segregationist and flash-frozen Cold Warrior Jesse Helms. If Louisiana enjoyed the hottest and the last of the red-hot poppas, North Carolina was perversely attached to the last of the ice-cold godfathers whose racial politics chilled the South for one hundred years. Jesse arrived in the Senate at the end of the war in Vietnam and left on the eve of the invasion of Iraq, thirty years during which neither he nor America appeared to learn anything at all. He was faithful to his wife, and also faithful to the apartheid National Party of South Africa, who probably kept Nelson Mandela in prison a few years longer because Helms offered secret support from Washington. He was just as faithful to his friend Roberto D'Aubuisson, the psychopathic Salvadoran death squad commander known as "Blowtorch Bob," whose thousands of victims included Archbishop Óscar Romero.

Jesse didn't steal, either. No one ever caught him with his pants down or with his hand in the cookie jar. But there was blood on that hand, and on the other hand, too, though Helms may well have been too stupid to understand where it came from. Is it any wonder that some of us in North Carolina would have preferred his contemporary Edwin Edwards, Sweeties and all, who taunted the Klan instead of courting it and counting on its vote? A politician's conscience—if that's not an oxymoron—can harbor things a whole lot worse than adultery.

And Who Will Lead Us?

THE PROBLEM WITH PRESIDENTS

2016

I was eating dinner with friends in a restaurant in Chevy Chase, circa 1990, when George Herbert Walker Bush and a small entourage walked across the dining room on the way to their table. Mr. Bush happened to be president of the United States at that time, and to my horror most of the diners broke into polite applause, many of them even rising from their chairs to honor the chief executive. I sensed that my friends—hardcore Democrats, both—were tempted to join in this modest ovation. Possibly they were inhibited by my presence and my sour frown of disapproval.

President George H. W. Bush had not achieved much worthy of applause that year, or any year as far as I was concerned. The clapping, I understood, was in deference to the office, not the man, and it was a part of capital culture I hadn't previously encountered. As a journalist I'd crossed paths with a couple of presidents, including G. H. W. Bush, but I had never been in a private place where a president appeared unexpectedly. I was mildly appalled, but also amused. When I was living in Edinburgh, one of the things I had admired about the British, and especially the Scots, was the way they treated their elected officials—with more impatience than courtesy, the way you might treat incompetent employees who need frequent dressings down to perform adequately. I remember my delight, and slight embarrassment, when the woman behind the counter at my fishmonger's berated the local MP one morning, haranguing the poor man mercilessly while he waited for his plaice. She put him in his plaice, if you'll forgive the pun. And the prime minister, the official closest to an American president in the UK's hierarchy, is no exception to this rich tradition of constituent abuse.

The former Prime Minister Tony Blair, whose great political and moral blunder was his support for the American invasion of Iraq, is considered a war criminal by a substantial minority of Britons. He's the target of a website that offers over £2,000 cash to anyone who attempts a citizen's arrest.

So far at least five citizens have collected, the most recent a bartender at the Tramshed restaurant in London. Blair's rude treatment by unforgiving countrymen is a source of amusement and curiosity in Great Britain, but precious little sympathy. "I think there's something about Blair that really makes a red mist descend upon people who would otherwise be able to judge more objectively," speculated a professor of politics at Queen Mary University.

It makes me sad to think of Blair pursued through Hyde Park by bartenders with homemade arrest warrants, while the American president who seduced and abandoned him (yet another Bush) is quietly building his library and scheming to revise his "legacy." Every law-abiding citizen is entitled to some personal dignity—but it's my firm belief that elected officials, even heads of state, are entitled to no more than the rest of us. When America elects some fatuous mediocrity to its highest office, why does it seem hardwired to treat him as if gravity and wisdom, even glamour, come along with the key to the White House?

That has been the great problem with the presidency. If Great Britain gets this right and the United States gets it wrong, it's in part because Britons can settle all their class deference, celebrity hunger, and patriotic sentiment on their queen. The throne is a purely ceremonial institution, a high empty office that in this day and age could hardly be occupied comfortably by anyone who was not a well-bred woman born in the 1920s. It may not have much of a future. But at the present it focuses all the population's archaic monarchist instincts on an actual monarch, leaving people free to treat politicians with no more respect than they deserve, as genuine democracy prescribes.

No one understood this better than George Washington—the great George Washington, to give this unusual man his due. He had barely defeated the armies of King George III when Tory elements here in the colonies urged him to become King George IV, or something very close to it. Washington recoiled. He was a natural democrat who demanded little deference and conspicuously offered little, not even to the God of his fathers. He attended Episcopalian services where he would neither kneel nor take Communion, an example I have followed patriotically.

Few ordinary mortals are as free of petty vanities as George Washington. In the early years of the republic the office of president rarely dwarfed the men who held it, a measure of the character and stature of the early presidents—most prominently Washington's neighbors, those slave-holding aristocrats from Virginia. And the stern Adamses of Boston, father and son, were descended from Puritans who held vanity to be a deadly sin. But the expanding suffrage of "Jacksonian" democracy, along with a flood of immigrants and the growth of cities, brought new kinds of politics to the fore, and new, much smaller kinds of politicians. The second half of the nineteenth century produced one memorable, larger-than-life president, and he was murdered by John Wilkes Booth. By the turn of the twentieth century, a template for our modern political system was in place. It wasn't very pretty, or very likely to place a giant or a genius in the White House.

"As democracy is perfected," wrote H. L. Mencken, American democracy's most savage critic, "the office of president represents, more and more closely, the inner soul of the people. On some great and glorious day the plain folks of the land will reach their heart's desire at last and the White House will be adorned by a downright moron." Mencken published that prediction in July 1920. Four months later, the plain folks elected Warren G. Harding, ranked by historians as one of the least intelligent, least virtuous of American presidents. Mencken, who coined the word "Gamaliese" (Gamaliel was Harding's middle name) to describe the mutilated syntax of the president's speeches, disrespected him so venomously that Harding's untimely death inspired him to write a sneering satire of the funeral train bearing the presidential remains on their final journey. The scandalized publisher of *The Smart Set* refused to print it, which ended Mencken's celebrated reign as the editor of that popular magazine.

Liberals have hailed the ascension of a "downright moron" as a prophecy of Ronald Reagan or either of the Bushes who succeeded him (Gerald Ford, no rocket scientist either, was never actually elected). But in all fairness, America's closest escape from Mencken's dire prediction was the presidential election of 2008. The Republican nominee John McCain, who would have made a notably elderly president, chose the bewilderingly underqualified, arguably simpleminded Sarah Palin as his vice presidential running mate, who in victory might have lurked that proverbial single "heartbeat" from the nation's highest office. Many of those plain folks Mencken despised still adore her; but I hope some of them read a recent news item reporting that the entire Palin family—mother, father, sister, and brother—had been restrained by police after turning an Alaska barbecue into a bloody brawl. Son Track was actually stripped to the waist and smeared with gore; daugh-

ter Bristol tried to drag a woman by her hair. It was a jaw-dropping re-
minder of how dreadfully low we can go when the democracy is inseparable
from the celebrity culture.

Heaven forbid that I should sound partisan here, but when the Republican Party adopted its Southern strategy, absorbing most of the Dixiecrats
alienated by the Voting Rights Act, it gained a lot of votes and sacrificed a lot
of SAT points. One decade ago, the winner of my Brutal Honesty Award was
Robert Brandon, chairman of the philosophy department at Duke University. When Duke was accused of excluding "conservatives" from its faculty,
Brandon replied, with good humor and little tact, "We try to hire the best,
smartest people available. If, as John Stuart Mill said, stupid people are generally conservative, then there are lots of conservatives we will never hire."

If you think you've already seen a lot of presidential candidates tailor-
made for the satire of H. L. Mencken or Comedy Central, just watch the
Republicans suit up for 2016. It's not clear whether Mill or Mencken is the
greatest prophet for our time. But it's worth considering whether the people who hold any president in the highest esteem—who will applaud and
genuflect when he enters the room—are the same ones who vote to make
presidents of the lowest charlatans and chumps. During the early months of
the 2012 primaries, when Donald Trump emerged briefly as the Republican
front-runner, I considered emigration to almost any place free of terrorists
and malaria. A patriot has to draw the line somewhere.

"In all my life," Mencken boasted, "I don't recall ever writing in praise of
a sitting president." To sum up the Calvin Coolidge presidency, he wrote,
"Nero fiddled, but Coolidge only snored." He called Woodrow Wilson a liar
and Franklin D. Roosevelt a fool. It was his nemesis Roosevelt who managed to retaliate, fittingly, against this cynic who jeered each president like
"a poor player that struts and frets his hour upon the stage." At the Grid-
iron Club dinner for Washington correspondents in 1934, Roosevelt rose
to read a vicious essay mocking the ignorance and incompetence of the
press—written years earlier by Mencken himself, who sat humiliated and
glowering a few tables away. FDR, like Abraham Lincoln, was a man elected
at a time of grave national crisis who grew into his oversized office, and became the inspirational leader no one could have foreseen. Unlike Lincoln,
he became the beloved King of America for which the presidency was originally and unfortunately designed. In the long run Mencken's pathological
loathing for Roosevelt harmed only Mencken, whose readers defected in
droves when he appeared to hate FDR more than Hitler.

Mencken was intemperate and held personal grudges, which he furiously denied. Yet no American writer ever dissected the presidency, in all its unfulfilled grandeur, its disappointments and diminishing returns, with more wit or insight. His essay "Imperial Purple," published in 1931, is the final word on presidential glamour and an antidote for all our latent royalist instincts. "All day long the right hon. lord of us all sits listening solemnly to bores and quacks," he wrote. "Twenty million voters with IQs below 60 have their ears glued to the radio; it takes four days' hard work to concoct a speech without a sensible word in it. Next day a dam must be opened somewhere. . . . The presidential automobile runs over a dog. It rains."

On the few occasions when they met, Franklin Delano Roosevelt—a droll gentleman himself—would call Mencken by his first name, Henry. Such an intimate address from a chief executive is an honor I can't claim. The first sitting president I encountered was Richard Nixon, the most dishonest and psychologically disfigured of them all. Almost encountered, to be exact. I was moving down the reception line at one of the "Newsmakers" parties my bosses at Time Inc. used to sponsor, a chance for editorial employees to meet some of the celebrities we wrote about. (At these events I also met Raquel Welch, Norman Mailer, Janis Joplin—whose date was the late albino bluesman Johnny Winter—and Joseph Stalin's daughter, Svetlana Alliluyeva.) At the end of the line, next to the publisher of *Time*, I spotted Nixon. I dropped out of the line and walked over to the buffet. My brother, a pacifist, was a draftee in Vietnam at that moment, and I had no stomach for shaking hands with Tricky Dick. This was an excess of youthful passion, as I look back on it now. I'd like to be able to tell you whether he had a limp handshake, sweaty palms, perhaps a shifty way of avoiding my eyes.

Jimmy Carter and George H. W. Bush were merely handshake (both firm) moments that yielded no insights, though I once had an enlightening conversation with George McGovern, who might have made an excellent president. The only president I met on multiple occasions—and even approached alone more than once—was the unsinkable Bill Clinton. These presidential meetings were an off-the-record privilege accorded to guests at the Renaissance New Year's conclaves at Hilton Head, South Carolina. My response to Bill Clinton was the same as everyone else's. I was charmed and impressed, and, like most journalists who meet him, unsettled by his aggressive intelligence. The Menckenized press is conditioned to condescend to politicians, an arrogance that's only rarely inappropriate. One New Year's

Eve, as I left the party, I shook Clinton's hand at the door, said good night, and sincerely wished him "Good luck." If memory serves me correctly, the Monica Lewinsky scandal was only two weeks away.

He weathered it, and the second presidential impeachment in American history, as he has weathered everything else. He ranks as the most gifted politician of his time, if not of all time. The electorate has forgiven, or forgotten, all his sins. In the polls his approval ratings are much higher than President Obama's—and consistently higher than Hillary's. Now the oddsmakers give him a better than 50–50 chance of reclaiming the White House, if only sideways as the husband of the first female president. Historian Douglas Brinkley compares him to "a snow leopard" for his amazing longevity at the highest altitudes of American politics. According to another historian, Julian Zelizer, "Clinton was the last president we've had who loved politics."

That's a mixed blessing, I'm afraid, and a questionable compliment. The political climate, even at "the highest altitudes," has taken a drastic turn for the worse since Mencken's day. The blizzards of attack ads aimed squarely at "voters with IQs below 60," the secret funding and truckloads of dirty money from sinister billionaires, the gross polarization and shameless video circus of modern elections might have shocked the cynic from Baltimore. We've built a sewer even politicians hate to swim in. Jimmy Carter, Barack Obama, and even George W. Bush have been criticized for squeamishness, of all things—for lacking the strong stomach required for the mud wrestling that power politics has become.

The presidency of the United States of America, a throne designed for a giant that is chronically dishonored by runts. The rest of the world waits anxiously, every four years, to see what kind of candidate will claim the prize. From the other side of a dysfunctional, dilapidated two-party system, we hear that Jeb is the best of the Bushes and the best of the Republicans—two pitifully modest claims. The Bushes, a dynasty of mediocrities, treat the American presidency like a rural sheriff's office that they can pass around from father to son to brother to son-in-law. Many simple Americans encourage them. The Bushes, like the Clintons, believe in personal and family destiny—and I'm not sure what else. A royal family is the last thing this stumbling republic needs now.

Goddess of Greed

AYN RAND IS THE RIGHT'S WEIRDEST IDOL OF ALL

2012

The Republican Party's slapstick search for a leader would be heartwarming and sidesplitting, but for the tragic knowledge that one of these scrambling Lilliputians will collect tens of millions of votes in the presidential election of 2012. Never have so many amounted to so little, talked so much rubbish, dreamed of an office so far above their abilities. Blood pressures rose among party elders when Donald Trump, marginally Republican and one of the greatest fools in the solar system, momentarily tossed his hairpiece into the ring and became the instant favorite. The GOP dilemma—a golden opportunity to rule but nothing to say and no one to say it—is so desperate that my instinct is to help them sort it out. Could we make a start, at least, by dismissing candidates who called for President Obama's birth certificate or raised the specter of sharia law in America, followed briskly off the stage by lunatics who dismiss global warming as a socialist plot? That would leave plenty of unbalanced extremists still in the running, yet reduce the stench of sheer evil and madness. The "Birther" and sharia cults reek of cheesy talk-radio racism; climate change denial is a stranger faith yet, a political assault on basic science that insults a ground squirrel's intelligence and casually threatens the survival of life on earth.

The party that produces Birthers and global-warming deniers no doubt harbors end-of-the-worlders, too, Christians who packed their bags for heaven with the senile prophet Harold Camping on May 21. Though none of them, I suppose, would commit to the time and expense of a presidential campaign just to preside over a nation of sinners expiring in fire and pestilence. Leo Rangell, the prominent Freudian analyst whose obituary is in this morning's *Times*, once lamented that the American public is "gullible or easily seduced, and susceptible to leaders of questionable character." Dr. Rangell wrote that in 1980, long before gullibility became such an epidemic that we began to doubt the value of our schools, before media demagogues made a billion-dollar industry of manipulating our most credulous citizens, before the Republican Party dedicated itself to gathering most of them into its fold. Before Rush Limbaugh, before Fox News, before the Tea Party.

"Finally, people's stupidity will break your heart," observed my father, a small-town politician and a loyal Republican of the moderate traditional strain that has been systematically exterminated by the radical Right. My father lived long enough to vote for George McGovern and against Ronald Reagan, but the rhetoric GOP candidates churn out to charm this Tea Party would sound extraterrestrial to most Republicans of his generation. The odious hypocrite Newt Gingrich, who considered himself a serious presidential candidate until his entire staff abandoned him in disgust, rests his appeal on his intellectual superiority to Sarah Palin and Rick Perry—a distinction much like being a faster runner than Dom DeLuise. In his obligatory precampaign book Gingrich claims that Barack Obama, a cautious centrist if there ever was one, drives a "secular-socialist machine" that "represents as great a threat to America as Nazi Germany or the Soviet Union once did."

Michael Savage, Rush Limbaugh, Father Coughlin, move over. Newt is just full of sharia, among other things, and accuses Obama of "Kenyan, anti-colonial behavior," a blatant pitch for the racist vote the Tea Party has reenergized. A colossal irony—demonstrating how hopelessly divided America has become—is that the radical philosopher Cornel West, a Black Princeton professor, calls Obama "a black mascot of Wall Street oligarchs and a black puppet of corporate plutocrats." This is not helpful of Dr. West, nor even responsible. He and Newt Gingrich are equally useless if a calmer, more logical and coherent political culture is what we're after. But if I had to say which of these two hostile portraits of our president is less preposterous, I'm sure I'd choose West's. Virtually all the valid criticism of Barack Obama has come from the Left.

When Tea-stained legislators gut environmental laws to protect corporate profits, when they sneer at climate change while America bakes in its bedrock like a big green casserole—when Republican educational reform means classrooms with fewer teachers and more guns—there's a temptation for reasonable Americans to throw up their hands and succumb to despair. Is it a death wish or a scheme to kill the rest of us, when "conservatives" fight against clean air laws, or legislate to place a loaded pistol in every yahoo's holster? I've reached the second half of my seventh decade, and I've never seen such an intimidating swarm of fanatics and fools marching under one banner. The election of a non-white president has brought out the worst in the worst of us. But who guessed that there were so many, or that their worst was so awful?

The late Albert Einstein, of my father's persuasion if not of his party, once wrote despairingly, "The tyranny of the ignoramuses is insurmountable and assured for all time." But the coalition that poisons this struggling republic is an unnatural one, made up of rich cynics who supply the money and poor ignoramuses who supply the votes. They have nothing in common, except that the cynics will say anything and the morons will believe it. There must be something, optimists insist, that could drive a wedge between the exploiters and the exploited—some irresistible revelation, some fraud or contradiction so flagrant that the most obtuse voters could see how callously and criminally they are being used.

How about Ayn Rand? The latest Republican poster boy, congressman Paul Ryan of Wisconsin, stole the media spotlight with a slash-to-the-bone budget proposal that Fox News heralded as the Magna Carta of fiscal responsibility in America. I lack the expertise to take on Rep. Ryan's budget digit for digit, but I place considerable confidence in the opinion of the *Times'* Paul Krugman, who won a Nobel Prize for Economics in 2008. "The proposal wasn't serious at all," Krugman wrote. "In fact, it was a sick joke. The only real things in it were savage cuts in aid to the needy and the uninsured, huge tax cuts for corporations and the rich, and Medicare privatization. All the alleged cost savings were pure fantasy." That sounds about par for the current Republican course, with fresh infusions of Tea Party belligerence and unreality. But what frightened me most about Rep. Ryan was the report that he is an avowed disciple of the writer/philosopher Ayn Rand, and has declared in public that Rand is "the reason I got involved in public service."

Good grief, she's back. She died in 1982, but someone neglected to drive a stake through her heart. A passion for the prose and philosophy of Ayn Rand tells us a great deal about an individual, none of it good. There are few surer signs of a poor reader, a poor thinker, and an unpleasant person than a well-thumbed copy of *Atlas Shrugged* or *The Fountainhead*. In 2005, Rand's acolytes gathered in Washington for a symposium to celebrate her one hundredth birthday—the occasion for Rep. Ryan's disturbing confession—and I admit I'd give anything to see the seating chart. If there was some way to ban everyone in that room from holding public office, we could probably turn the United States of America back toward the generous light of reason.

Yet Rand herself claimed that reason was her only guide. Who is/was Ayn Rand? (To parody the famous first line of *Atlas Shrugged*, "Who is John Galt?") Fifty years ago, when I first heard her name, that question was seldom asked. She was a major cultural figure, if not exactly a revered one. Critics despised her bestselling novels, and philosophers ridiculed her "objectivist" philosophy. She was to literature what Rod McKuen was to poetry, what Fabian was to rock 'n' roll, what Guru Maharaj Ji was to religion. Look them up. Like them, she once enjoyed a huge audience of admirers. Unlike them, she was never harmless and she's enjoying an alarming revival.

Since *Atlas Shrugged* was published in 1957, it has sold seven million copies. It's possibly the most polarizing book ever written. For every Paul Ryan who finds it life-shaping, a dozen readers are mystified and a dozen more appalled. Few actually finish the 1,200-page novel, which ends with the mysterious Galt drawing a dollar sign in the air with his finger. If you wade into this stuff up to your ankles—the hokey melodrama, the backlit macrocharacters posed like Easter Island monoliths, the cruel and obvious message stamped on every page—you begin to fear that you can never wash it off.

At times her critics oversimplify Rand's beliefs, which embody any number of contradictions and opacities. But essentially she glorifies the will and celebrates Nietzsche's Übermensch, the superman whose blazing passage through the world need never be impeded by the interests or opinions of mediocrities like you and me. It's the same string of arrogant assumptions that spawned the Master Race theories of Herr Hitler: ego-deification, social Darwinism, arbitrary stratification of human types. Adapted for capitalism, it becomes the divine right to plunder—a license for those who own nearly everything to take the rest, because they wish to, because they can. Because the weak don't matter. Let the big dogs feed.

This repulsive theology was the work of a fairly repulsive person. For an eyewitness portrait of Ayn Rand in the flesh, in the prime of her celebrity, you can't improve on the "Übermensch" chapter in Tobias Wolff's autobiographical novel *Old School*. Invited to meet with the faculty and student writers at the narrator's boarding school, Rand arrives with an entourage of chain-smoking idolaters in black and behaves so repellently that her audience of innocents gets a life lesson in what kind of adult to avoid, and to avoid becoming. Rude, dismissive, vain, and self-infatuated to the point of obtuseness—she names *Atlas Shrugged* as the only great American novel—Rand and her hissing chorus in black manage to alienate the entire school, even the rich board member who had admired and invited her.

What strikes Wolff's narrator most forcefully is her utter lack of charity or empathy, her transparent disgust with everything she views as disfiguring or disabling: a huge wen on the headmaster's forehead, the narrator's running head cold, the war injury that emasculated Hemingway's Jake Barnes in *The Sun Also Rises*. To the boy, she appears to be exactly the sort of merciless egotist who might have designed a fascist philosophy that exalts power and disparages altruism. Rand is wearing a gold pin in the shape of a dollar sign. After meeting her, he can no longer read a word of *The Fountainhead*, which as an adolescent romantic he had enjoyed.

This division of the human race into the elect few who are destiny's darlings and the "second-rate" multitudes above whom they soar—this Übermensch nonsense—is perilously thin ice on which to rest a philosophy (Nietzsche, you recall, went hopelessly mad). Since there's no agency that rates human beings the way we rate bonds, the elect are always *self-elected* supermen and superwomen. Super, says who? If it's supposed to be intellect as much as will that sets them above us, I sense a critical problem. Whenever individuals of superior intelligence begin to comprehend the human condition, the first fruits of knowledge are humility and irony—those two things Rand and her heroes most spectacularly lack. Personally, I never feel more superior than when I see someone carrying a copy of *Atlas Shrugged*. What actually sets the self-styled super race apart is an unrepressed infantile id, a raging "I want" that defies socialization. These are damaged children, people of arrested development drawn to an ugly philosophy that legitimizes narcissism and socially unacceptable behavior. Donald Trump would be a perfect example.

For an apostle of self-willed happiness, the goddess of greed led a troubled life, marked by depressions, amphetamine addiction, messy love affairs, and betrayals. But you could say that she had a capacious mind, if not a healthy or an orderly one. She was well educated, she had actually read Aristotle and Nietzsche before she hobbled them and hitched them to her wagon. Her unlikely twenty-first-century resurrection is the work of much smaller, often almost invisible minds that cherry-pick the vast creaking structure of her oeuvre for their own ends, just as they cherry-pick the Bible or *The Wealth of Nations*.

If corporate feudalism is your dream for America, she's the prophet for you. Her naive faith in capitalism and contempt for "the welfare state" are just what the right-wing doctor ordered. Much of the rest, alas, will never fly in Alabama. Pundits have been delighted to note that the heroine of the new Republicans was a pacifist who opposed the Vietnam War, a feminist who supported abortion, an adulteress who preached free love, a bohemian who mocked family life and childbearing, an elitist who sneered at the common man, and, after all her "nanny state" rhetoric, a recipient of Social Security and Medicare and a late, sick convert to the benefits of socialized medicine.

Worst of all, for Tea-stained Christian Republicans, she was a militant atheist. In Rand's ideology, religious faith was the most abject form of weakness, a sniveling retreat from the hardheaded, self-centered "objectivism" her heroes impose on the world. She not only would have rejected Jesus and his gospels, she actually did—repeatedly. Christ's message that the poor are blessed and the meek will inherit the earth is antithetical to Rand's belief that the poor and meek are no more than mulch where the dreams of the mighty take root. So adamantly did she denounce the altruism and self-sacrifice at the center of the Christian message, it's no exaggeration to call her the intellectual Antichrist. It's no great exaggeration to say that praising her is like spitting in Christ's face.

How do Paul Ryan, Ron and Rand Paul, and company manage to pass off this radical atheist, this subversive Russian Jew (born Alissa Rosenbaum), as an iconic role model for Christian conservatives? Apparently they don't think they need to get into the details, not with their particular constituency. Assuming that they know the details themselves. The careless condescension of their leaders is not yet a scandal to the tea baggers of America's unlettered hard Right. But Ayn Rand seems like the biggest joke of all, one that might yet blow up in the party's face. The plutocrats she worshiped are so few, the plebeians she scorned are so many. The GOP's little people can't all be totally illiterate, and Limbaugh and Glenn Beck actually urge them to read this woman's books.

It's in-your-face deception that reminds me of the old stage villain, the silent-movie heavy with the waxed mustache, cackling behind his cloak and inviting the audience to share the cruelty he's about to inflict on his innocent victims. It's as if Wall Street is surreptitiously giving the finger to Main Street Republicans, laughing at the gullible recruits as they march to the polls to lower corporate taxes and deregulate markets. Ayn Rand, indeed. She would have applauded the big dogs' ruthlessness but rolled her eyes at the Christian-family rhetoric they're obliged to use for bait.

She wasn't one of them, of course; she certainly wasn't one of us. She was one of a kind, thank god. In her defense, you might argue that her love affair with capitalism was rooted in a Russian Jew's horror of the totalitarian systems that devastated Europe in the twentieth century. That offers her a gravitas she doesn't share with ultra-light Midwestern reactionaries like Paul Ryan or Michele Bachmann. But the more Americans read her books, the better for liberals and the worse, I think, for Republicans. Her work illustrates conclusively what a few brave clergymen and a few ink-stained relics like me have been saying for years to anyone who would listen, and to Republicans who refuse to listen—that Christianity and the wolverine capitalism of a John Galt are totally incompatible systems, two mutually exclusive human possibilities. They cancel each other out. Any political party that pretends to integrate them is a party of liars, and doomed.

Chaos Theory

WHEN MADNESS GAINS MOMENTUM

2020

To many American observers, writing in what they believe are safe offices on the eighteenth floor, condescend inappropriately to "failed states" like Haiti where armed gangs control the streets, where government and public safety have broken down and seem unlikely to be restored. Americans have no reason to be smug. The Capitol insurrection last January 6 occurred in exactly the same spirit of mob violence and incoherent protest as the current upheavals in Haiti, Cuba, and South Africa. There are neighborhoods in Chicago that are no safer than the streets of Port-au-Prince. Over the Fourth of July weekend, Chicagoans celebrated their nation's birthday in their special way—by shooting each other. One hundred people were shot, eighteen fatally, over the long holiday in the Windy City. The hospitalized victims included a police officer and two federal agents from the Bureau of Alcohol, Tobacco, Firearms and Explosives. So far this year there have been thirty-six shootings of Chicago police officers, six of them and counting in the month of July.

In the nation's capital, a major-league baseball game was suspended and postponed after gunshots from a drive-by skirmish (three wounded) outside the ballpark sent players fleeing the field to the safety of the visitors' clubhouse. The question is whether we're on the verge of chaos, or in the midst of it. Two blocks from my house in the quiet, Democratic-leaning village of Hillsborough, North Carolina, a downscale bar was recently exposed as a sort of clubhouse for a dozen members of the Proud Boys, one of the White Power militias that joined in the ransacking of the Capitol building. The Proud Boys even wear uniforms identifying themselves, but the owner of their chosen saloon refuses to ban them from the premises because so far they've done nothing wrong—they don't dare, he explained to a reporter, because at least half of them are on parole.

A thousand miles north in New England, where we had fled to escape the heat, Massachusetts state troopers encountered another alarming face of America's belligerent polarization. They pulled over a suspicious-looking van and found it occupied by eleven members of a Black militia called Rise of the Moors, all heavily armed and in full combat gear, as if they were driving to a revolution. The Moors, whose beliefs combine Black nationalism and aspects of Islam, explained that they were on their way to Bangor, Maine, to "train."

It turned out that none of the Moors' weapons were legally purchased, and that they boasted no valid driver's licenses, either. The authorities are still trying to sort out the purpose of their mission. On the other coast of this disintegrating republic, in California, two men with connections to the Proud Boys and another white paramilitary group called the Three Percenters were arrested for plotting to blow up the state's Democratic Party headquarters in Sacramento. In the home and business of one suspect, Ian Benjamin Rogers, police found fifty firearms, thousands of rounds of ammunition, and five pipe bombs. "I want to blow up a Democratic building bad," Rogers had texted his coconspirator. Other texts between them mentioned a scheme to kidnap or assassinate the liberal Jewish billionaire George Soros.

You don't have to be paranoid to conclude that there's no place to hide from armed and violent Americans, including citizens whose cognitive wiring has suffered irreparable meltdown. Among other signs of rapid civic decline that seemed to accompany the Covid-19 pandemic was an alarming increase in attacks on Asians, Blacks, and Jews by rabid white men. What constitutes a "failed state"? I think a fair definition would be any nation where the government is no longer able, willing, or interested in protecting its citizens from each other. If the United States of America has joined the sorry and growing roster of failed states, when and why did we turn the corner toward anarchy? I'd argue that the last pretense of civilization disappeared when military assault weapons were legalized for civilians, and an insane minority of Americans purchased a lion's share of all the functional firearms on the planet Earth, roughly four hundred million at last count.

Future historians writing our national obituary, "The Rise and Fall of the American Empire," would be flying blind if they didn't highlight the lethal role of the National Rifle Association, the once-innocuous "sportsman's club" that evolved into what Southern novelist William Styron denounced as "one of the most evil organizations to exist in any nation, past or present." Of course there's plenty of blame to pass around. The Democratic Left, pharisaic and often lemminglike in its ideological conformity, can appear irrelevant or worse when it throws its weight behind something like "Abolish the Police" at a point in our violent decline when we seem to need a dozen policemen patrolling every city block. Systemic racism is America's ancient curse, and Black Lives Matter is a rational response to its agonies. But pretending that all criminals and inmates are victims and all peace officers part of some official racist gestapo is no sane route to our salvation.

When a powerful nation slides toward dystopia, there's generally folly on all sides. But let's not pretend that responsibility is equally distributed. I have friends who claim to see no difference between Democrats and Republicans, but in fact that difference has never been greater. Nearly all Democrats and left-of-center independents vote to protect the vulnerable and the environment, eliminate the grossest inequities in the American system, and throttle, if possible, the winner-takes-all capitalism that has hand-delivered most of our wealth and power to a corporate plutocracy. That doesn't make them all wise and generous—except in contrast to their hostile rivals on the Right.

If there's a single dominant reason for America's descent into raging incoherence, it's the appalling putrefaction of a major political party, a condition confirmed in Washington on January 6. For fifty years the Republicans have been straining to the right, but that movement accelerated so rapidly in the past couple of decades that the party's electoral power now rests entirely on the votes of the bigoted, benighted, and belligerent—those Killer B's. Once the party of emancipation, it's now the party of white nationalists and Jim Crow–style crusades against voting rights. The GOP "base," white, angry, and tragically, heartrendingly, mind-bendingly stupid, worships Donald Trump, and to please him it's more than ready to rip a once-admired democracy up by its roots. When Dick Cheney's daughter is your last voice of reason and moderation, friend, your party is way down the road that led Germany to swastikas and jackboots.

Personally I'd never use that other f-word, *fascist*, in polite discourse—so I leave that escalation to astute foreign observers. "The most dangerous threat facing the world is the transformation of the Republican Party in the US into a fascist movement," writes the Irish journalist Patrick Cockburn. In support of Cockburn's warning, the London-based Canadian columnist Gwynne Dyer writes, "Fascists do not have horns and a tail. They are mostly ordinary people who believe that they will lose something vitally important (their wealth, their status, their values) if they do not break the rules and take over. The changing demography of the United States means that the Republicans will lose almost every election in the future if they don't seize power now. They are not planning death camps or world conquest, but they have become fascists, and they will not be good neighbors."

The party of middle-American schoolteachers and farmers has become the party of Proud Boys and neo-Nazis. General Mark Milley, the chairman of the Joint Chiefs of Staff who has emerged as a Trump-resisting hero in several new books about the last agonies of postelection Trumpworld, recognized the January 6 insurrectionists for what they were: "These are the same people we fought in World War II," he told his staff.

I try to imagine what my late father, a WWII naval officer and a good (liberal) Republican all his life, might make of a GOP of potential storm troopers who would have scared the hell out of General Eisenhower and maybe even Richard Nixon. There seem to be tens of millions of these twenty-first-century neo-Republicans, and they're not just exasperating us and blocking any hope we might entertain of fair and rational government in this country. They're also killing us—many of the rest of us—quite literally.

Consider, first, our four years under a Trump administration that barred its officials from using the words "climate change" (and now we have hellfire in Oregon, 110-plus temperatures in British Columbia and Siberia). Second, the right wing's crazy politicization of the Covid-19 vaccine, which is filling hospitals at this moment, and third, the GOP's blind alliance with the NRA, which insists that every lunatic, felon, and brooding loner should own all the deadly weapons his homicidal heart desires. Contemplate the eventual body count. The Fourth Horseman of the Republican Apocalypse is, of course, the demented ex-president, a coarse, profane bully deep in the late stages of cognitive disintegration.

Among the revelations from this summer's wave of books offering Trump postmortems—along with the fact that the ex-president uses the F-word almost constantly—is the consensus from alienated administration officials and even White House insiders that Trump is mentally ill. Sadly, they seem to have known it all along. "Unhinged," "deranged," and "off his rocker" are among their verdicts. I can't resist boasting that I told you this all along, as far back as 2015, when I polled a couple of Georgetown psychiatrists and reported their diagnoses in this publication. Michael Wolff, whose book *Landslide: The Final Days of the Trump Presidency* comes out this week, concludes that Trump has "completely departed reality."

You didn't need a degree in psychiatry to recognize that this man is nuts. What's shocking is that so many knew it, and kept it a secret to retain their Republican credentials. But the most competent ones seem to have abandoned him. *The Washington Post* journalists Yasmeen Abutaleb and Damian Paletta, whose new Trump book is titled *Nightmare Scenario*, write that his administration, at the time the pandemic struck, was staffed mostly by "a mix of family members, 20-somethings, hangers-on, fourth stringers, former lobbyists, sycophants."

This team of ciphers and losers was running the United States when it faced one of the greatest threats and challenges in its history. I guess that's what it means to be a "failed state." *Nightmare Scenario* chronicles that failure.

But Donald Trump was the past—we pray to God—and most of us still hope to live a little way into the future, even in a failed state, even with the mess he leaves behind. It seems possible that we could weather one insane, incompetent president and regain our balance. Joe Biden hopes so. But what scares me even more than the memory of an awful presidency—one new book reports that Trump told his aides we should "just shoot" civil rights protesters—is this QAnon cult that deifies Trump as the messiah of a violent new religion. You have to be stark raving mad to subscribe to QAnon, which is silly sci-fi conspiracy loaded with hatred, anti-Semitism, and psychotic demonization of Democrats. Was there ever even one pedophile who was also a Satanist, and a Democrat? But I read somewhere that 15 percent of American adults—thirty million?—believe in at least some part of QAnon's theology. There are forty QAnon candidates, all Republicans of course, for the 118th Congress.

QAnon believers are totally on board for the violent overthrow of the government, and the ex-con, ex-Trump aide General Michael Flynn is ready to lead the charge if Trump isn't up to it. Democracy depends entirely on getting actual facts to the voters—and on educating the voters to recognize the facts, and the fiction, when they see them. The very existence of QAnon seems to indicate that the United States is failing on both scores, and on a critical scale.

"So how did we end up here?" asks Paul Krugman in *The New York Times*. "How did one of our two major political parties come not only to reject democracy, but to exalt ignorance and despise competence of any kind? I don't know, but if you aren't terrified, you aren't paying attention."

Failed state or fascist state? Now there's a choice to ponder.

From the Madhouse
to the White House

THE STRAITJACKET BLUES

2019

> Let's not mince words here: The President
> of the United States is a nut job.
> —George Conway, August 10, 2019

There are no more words to mince. And the fact that the author of this warning is married to and cohabits amiably with KellyAnne Conway, whose loathsome job is to defend and interpret the nut job in question, makes you wonder whether George himself can be in full command of his faculties. Or, frankly, whether any of us Americans can still claim to be functioning as rational adults. Where's a well-lighted path out of this?

The political labyrinth in which we seem lost is like nothing this country has ever seen before—certainly like nothing I've seen before, and I've been a working journalist since 1967.

"Politics, as we see at the moment, are grubby, dishonest and chaotic," said the English writer Penny Junor, lamenting the state of things in Brexit-torn Britain. If only those adjectives were the worst ones we could apply to the circus now playing in Washington, DC. The impeachment of Donald Trump by the House of Representatives has been a litmus test for political animals, revealing depths of depravity and dishonesty the most cynical observer would have hesitated to credit, a few short years ago. A parade of eminently credible, sometimes eloquent witnesses has indicted the president beyond any shadow of reasonable doubt. There's no question in any sane person's mind that he did exactly what he stands accused of, that he tried to bribe Ukrainian officials (with our tax money) to find information damaging to Joe Biden, a political rival. If this is an impeachable crime, as most constitutional scholars believe, Donald Trump should soon be nothing but an ugly memory, a few long strands of nasty, lacquered orange hair on the furniture in the Oval Office. Any sane president, hearing this testimony against him, would already have resigned. But no sane president would have stepped into such a slimy business to begin with.

George Conway is not a psychiatrist, but many professionals in that field have already weighed in on the president's cognitive decline, and the consensus is alarming. If he were a more appealing, amiable individual, like Ronald Reagan long after his cerebral warranty had expired, I might feel sympathy for Donald Trump. He's almost my age, an age at which the specter of senility is no joking matter. But Trump is and has always been such a vain, cruel, mean-spirited featherweight of a man that the eclipse of what we call his mind is tragic only in its possible consequences, for Americans and for a world community that stares astonished at what our foundering political system has produced.

A party that long since sacrificed principle to power and profits has made a president out of one of the most corrupt, ridiculous, and ultimately disgusting individuals in my entire generation, and senile dementia or some more urgent form of mental illness has consumed his meager resources right in front of our eyes.

It's a pitiful spectacle, played out hour by hour, absurdity upon absurdity, on this perversion of a medium they used to call Twitter. But Donald Trump, nearly three years into the farce of his presidency, is an established, predictable disaster. Or obscenity, if you will. He has taken "The Swamp" he promised to drain and turned it into an open sewer with a transatlantic stench that reaches far beyond the Ukrainian steppes. What the impeachment process has revealed anew is the colossal cynicism and dishonesty of the president's supporters. Certain Texas legislators, according to the late Molly Ivins, were the intellectual equals of houseplants and root vegetables, and I understand that many congressional Republicans were spawned in that same gene pool. Still, I refuse to believe that anyone now in Congress is so dim and befuddled that he honestly believes the president is innocent, or mentally intact either. These people all know he's nuts, that he's a delusional thug whose fantasy avatars range from Mussolini to Tony Soprano. Yet they fight for him fiercely on the floor of the House of Representatives, and the Republican Party has just committed another $7 million to defend him from the Ukrainian impeachment.

They're all in for a presidency where the lights are all out, morally and functionally, where the kind of megalomania common to back wards and padded cells has become the bewildering norm. It should have been all over but the sniggering when Trump declared himself "a stable genius." There should have been a kind but firm way to escort him from the White House to a place where he could get the care and medication that might stabilize his condition. Yet through it all—the Mueller report, the preposterous turnover among his staff and appointees, the seventy thousand refugee children he incarcerated, the rumors of sexual assaults, the aides and associates imprisoned, the weird racist outbursts and now the Ukrainian fiasco—his support in Congress and among voters of the proverbial Republican "base" remains steady.

What do these loyalists tell themselves, that a rational person could understand? There are the personally compromised, of course, an expanding roster of amoral lackeys that now appears to include the vice president and the secretary of state. There are the congenitally cynical and greedy, who always vote their wallets and know that any Republican plutocrat, no matter how vile, will help them to maximize their fortunes. These reliable allies add up to a relatively small minority. It's the rest of Trump's steady 40 percent, the majority that isn't wealthy and is nowhere close to the sources of power, that keeps us scratching our heads. What holds this "base" in place? Is it possible for a reasonably informed citizen to dismiss the entire impeachment cycle as a predictable partisan squabble, just another sore-loser attempt to dislodge the brash New Yorker who shot down Hillary Clinton?

The key phrase, I'm afraid, is "reasonably informed." Polls show that loyalists get nearly all their news of the world and the nation from this thing on TV called Fox News, which at its best is a Republican propaganda machine, at its worst an exercise in police-state mind control that Joseph Goebbels would have envied. The president's incestuous relationship with Fox is an unprecedented scandal—he recruits staff from its ideologues and turns to them for advice and solace—and some of the praise its "journalists" heap upon our imaginary dictator would mortify Kim Jong Un. Trump recently boasted that Lou Dobbs of Fox Business had anointed him "the greatest president in the history of our country, including George Washington and Abraham Lincoln."

Surely not, Lou? Did Trump make this up? But Dobbs is our age—mine and the president's—and if this is his take on American history I'm afraid that his own senile dementia is well advanced. With the invaluable help of Fox extremists like Dobbs, Sean Hannity (who to his credit has never claimed to be a journalist), Tucker Carlson, and Laura Ingraham, the far right feeds truckloads of such banana-republic nonsense to the helplessly gullible. Trump's approval ratings indicate that it's highly effective. With Fox, right-wing radio, and a wild array of reactionary websites and social media cliques mobilized to misinform them, it's now possible for American voters to bypass reality altogether. They can fantasize a world that conforms perfectly to their prejudices and see it reflected in a hundred mirrors. When the history of the twenty-first century is written, this flight from facts and a president's attacks on "fake news"—anything printed or broadcast that didn't flatter him—may be the historians' dominant theme.

Fox and its friends have succeeded in changing the meaning of the word "conservative," as it applies to politics. As a rural, hardcore Luddite with Republican roots, a not-so-closeted libertarian and a pragmatist with no great faith in the socialist dream, I used to think I qualified as conservative. In 2020 I pass for a superannuated Bolshevik; *conservative* is a word reserved for malignant Neanderthal conspiracy peddlers like Alex Jones, or presidential advisors in the lineage of Steve Bannon and Stephen Miller, dark figures who consort with white supremacists and Holocaust deniers. Don't write to tell me that Miller is Jewish. His own uncle has denounced him for anti-immigrant hypocrisy and pandering to anti-Semites of the alt-right. In Trumpworld this scent of madness, of contradictory outer-fringe eccentricity, is always near at hand. The president's personal attorney for impeachment strategy, Jay Sekulow, is the former general counsel for Jews for Jesus. He's a protégé of the "prosperity gospel" evangelists Paul and Janice Crouch, who introduced him on their TV show as "our little Jew."

You couldn't make this stuff up. ("Good grief," as Charlie Brown used to say.) Another apostle of the prosperity gospel, Paula White, is Trump's newly appointed religious guru and liaison to the evangelical community. The unholy alliance between the vulgar, profane, almost certainly criminal president and the most sanctimonious fundamentalists must be one of the weirdest in political history. Energy Secretary Rick Perry, another sad stooge who sold his soul to Trump, has actually referred to the Great Orange Sinner as "the chosen one."

Which is the point where your head begins to spin, your mouth goes dry, and your teeth begin to grind involuntarily. Trump was too crazy for those multistarred generals whose medals and machismo he worshipped like a little boy; he was too crazy for Rex Tillerson, the CEO of Exxon Mobil, whose appointment as secretary of state signaled this administration's abject submission to the fossil fuel industry and climate change denial. He was too crazy even for John Bolton, the most bloodthirsty, warmongering antidiplomat in the Republican arsenal. But he's not too crazy, polls continually remind us, for the poor double-mortgaged, credit-maxed schmuck in one of the "flyover" states like my own, who absorbs and consecrates the ugly xenophobic drivel with which the Hannitys and Limbaughs pollute the airwaves. There are tens of millions of these red-state underdogs, the same polls remind us, who never seem to grasp that there's nothing for them in the Republican cupboard, no substance in the promises of a fat racist liar in a forty-inch necktie.

Donald Trump's imminent impeachment will not result in his removal from office. He will not be remanded to an appropriate nursing home or asylum. He'll be rebuked and humiliated, in our terms, but humiliation is a meaningless concept to a demented hustler with no more shame than the hungry fox who breaks into your henhouse. He'll retain the support of nearly all the Republicans in Congress, a once-flexible coalition that's become little more than a white nationalist cabal. He'll be nominated to run for a second term, with an enormous treasure chest, and there are reputable insiders who think he may win again. With his fourteen thousand fact-checked lies in one thousand days and his revolving-door dream team of felons, fanatics, lobbyists, predatory billionaires, and doddering freelance incompetents like Rudy Giuliani, he'll continue to make a sorry mockery of representative democracy. Columnist Leonard Pitts reminded us that John Dean told Richard Nixon, during the Watergate scandal, that there was "a cancer on the presidency." "But in 2019," Pitts added, "the cancer is the presidency."

What is a sane patriot supposed to do—tear up his passport, join a survivalist militia, research real estate in Saskatchewan? America's suicide rate has gone up 30 percent in the twenty-first century; last month in Maine, a wealthy couple my age, in fair health but deeply discouraged by the state of things, left explanatory messages for their friends and family and took a lot of sleeping pills together, dying hand in hand.

Don't pursue this option, please. Or if you must, please wait until after you've voted in the presidential election. The dead don't vote—at least in most precincts—and the Democrats who hope to dislodge Donald Trump need every sane voter who can breathe. It doesn't really matter which Democrat is chosen from this multifaced, multiflawed lineup of candidates. This is not the time for the Democratic Party to indulge in its traditional cannibalism; I can't even bear to watch them attack each other. The only thing that matters in 2020 is evicting this sick, this awful, this destructively evil man from the White House. On every truly urgent issue, every question of survival America faces—climate change, gun control, environmental degradation, income inequality, poverty—his lunatic administration is either doing nothing or working hard to make things worse. Review those issues and consider that these people are quite literally killing us—you and me, our children and grandchildren. Defeating Trump is not a goal that hinges on our political philosophies. It's literally a matter of life and death.

Slaughterhouse America

REMEMBER THE ALAMO?

2022

As a onetime columnist for the *Buffalo Evening News*, I had been working on an appropriate response to the racist massacre in Buffalo. But I hadn't made much progress when the Buffalo atrocities were upstaged, only ten days later, by the wholesale slaughter of schoolchildren in Uvalde, Texas, which cost twice as many innocent lives. There are times, becoming more frequent, when no one outside our national community knows what to make of America.

Even some of us natives are beginning to wonder if there's any way forward, or even any way to explain ourselves to our neighbors. Two almost concurrent mass murders by deranged teenage loners, both armed with legally purchased assault rifles, naturally spurred sane legislators and officeholders to renew their demands for effective gun control, that ever-elusive goal here in Earth's arsenal with its four hundred million civilian-owned firearms. But what's left to say, that wasn't said after Newtown, after Parkland, after any of the scores of mass murders (270 since 2009) that occur here and virtually nowhere else on the planet? School shootings—a kind of imitative, competitive way for floridly insane teenagers to commit suicide—are such a bizarre nightmare feature of life in America that no dystopian novelist could have made them up. There have been twenty-seven this year, and counting.

(Morning in America, June 3, 2022, front page headlines:
New York Times—"Mass Shootings Just Won't Stop: 20 in Nine Days"
Raleigh News and Observer—"NC Had Info on Over 250 Planned School Attacks")

No marginally civilized country would ever allow civilians to own military-style assault weapons, the weapons of choice for mass murderers. It's been reported that America's "hunters" now own more of them than its army. Pistols? Fifty years ago Supreme Court Justice William O. Douglas endorsed restricting them to law enforcement officers. No doubt he was right, and back in 1960 60 percent of Americans agreed with him. Today, after decades of deadly brainwashing by the gun lobby, only 19 percent would support a pistol ban. Our ballistic passions are unique. Open carry and concealed carry rights sound like science fiction to anyone but an American. In a country with any hope of protecting its children from homicidal psychos, paranoid home defenders would have to pretend to be hunters, and also required to keep their rifles and shotguns under lock and key.

In all the world beyond America's exotic gun cult, that's logic in its simplest, starkest form. Arguing against it is dangerous and ridiculous. But tell that to the Republicans. Locked in a sexual embrace with the National Rifle Association, reduced to prostitution by the NRA's largesse, the Republican Party finds itself morally paralyzed—blind to reason, blind to irony, blind to shame. The massacres in Buffalo and Uvalde should be a final litmus test of the GOP's humanity. If it can shrug off the memory of those murdered children and still refuse to move the needle one degree in the direction of saner gun control, it has no place left to hide its shameful, pitiful bondage to the bullet merchants. And this faltering republic it pollutes, on life support since the election of Donald Trump in 2016, will have slipped into a coma from which we may not recover.

Gun control is the argument we never lose, the battle we never win. In this pay-to-play political system we like to call a democracy, no pressure group has maximized its resources half as effectively as the gun lobby. Though only 30 percent of American adults are gun owners—and a significant percentage of them are not Second Amendment extremists—the NRA and its shock troops cast the biggest legislative shadow of any weird minority on earth. In many red states, a politician who opposes them commits political suicide. The arms industry and its lobbyists couldn't have done it, of course, without a certain strain of primitive belligerence that always lurked in America's bloodstream. It's up to psychiatrists to explain the malignant blend of machismo and paranoia that created our gun cult. But we all have neighbors whose idea of freedom is an AR-15 in every pickup.

The egregious Texas governor Greg Abbott, who in the past year signed twenty-two laws loosening gun restrictions, surveyed the slaughter in Uvalde and blamed it on pure "evil," as if it had been some incarnate demon pumping lead into the bodies of cowering children. No, governor—it was a mad person, an insane boy who had taken psychosis to its furthest human extreme. Even prosecuting him as a criminal and executing him would have been an empty charade. A permanent padded cell is the only safe place for a lunatic who mows down third graders in cold blood. "Evil" is the NRA, once denounced by the novelist William Styron as "one of the most evil organizations to exist in any nation, past or present."

"Evil" is a political system—specifically Republicans like Abbott—that enabled this mad boy to buy an assault rifle at the age of eighteen. You can identify the gun cult's most abject slaves by the mindless prefab slogans these officials recite after every massacre: "law-abiding citizens," "a good guy with a gun," "guns don't kill people..." etc. Even the holy Second Amendment is a laughable pretense, as if something authored by men in powdered wigs, in the days of hostile Indians and muzzleloaders, retains any relevance in the age of AR-15s and shoulder-mounted rocket launchers.

In a country where one hundred people die of bullet wounds every day, new gun laws are a simple matter of life and death—literally—and the people who oppose them have innocent blood on their hands. Buckets of it, lately. But outrageously easy access to deadly weapons is not the only factor in the terror that's turning a prideful republic into a reeking slaughterhouse. It's true that the entertainment media—TV, movies, video games—are rotten with gun violence. But in the long run a more psychologically damaging influence may be the vaunted internet and its deformed offspring, the social media.

The internet snake pits, the racist and neo-Nazi sites, and conspiracy factories have poisoned the brains of millions of Americans of all ages. But it's the younger generations who appear to have the most disturbing online addictions. The racist assassin in Buffalo was a total creature of the internet. According to *The New York Times*, he "surfed through a smorgasbord of racist and anti-Semitic websites online. . . . He lingered in furtive chat rooms on Reddit and 4chan. . . . He toggled between 'documentaries' on extremist websites and gun tutorials on YouTube." And I can testify that the psychotic racism that resulted in the deaths of ten Black people was fed only by his online experience. He was from Conklin, New York. I grew up in an almost identical small town in the northern Appalachians, where there was no racial tension because there were almost no African Americans.

Half an hour before the massacre in Uvalde, the shooter declared his intentions on three social media posts. On the day he bought his assault rifles, he sent a photo of them to another Instagram user in Europe, a woman he was trying to impress. The Buffalo shooter was live streaming online when he opened fire, for god's sake. When I read these things I can't help thinking about all the "influencers" and Instagram and TikTok "stars" and "superstars" who are making a living, and fortunes in some cases, by feeding personal content to thousands and even millions of "followers" online. Performance. These young people are performing. They're living their lives in front of an audience. This seems pretty crazy, at least to those of us from the prewired generations. It seems pathological. And when online performance is a norm for sad losers who are already profoundly crazy, some may become assassins who know that only a school massacre will ever make a big enough impression online.

A few of us can remember when only politicians and entertainers needed an audience, and when we thought the most effective and admirable people were the ones who called the least attention to themselves. Pardon my antiquity. Clearly the world has changed, though not in many ways that I applaud. When did privacy become archaic? Of all the extremes that mark the generation gap, performance culture may turn out to be the most alarming and tenacious. We can change our crazy gun laws if a terrified unarmed majority can find a will and a way to flex its electoral muscle. But this strange compulsion to perform your life for an online audience has printed a couple of generations with pathological needs and vulnerabilities their parents could never imagine.

Most of the shooters belong to these generations. They're males under twenty-five. If that's the way the demographics keep trending, banning AR-15s might not be enough to save the schoolchildren. The conventional wisdom about the internet and its ugly children is that we can never turn back—technology is a one-way street. If that's the case, and I don't doubt it, it's going to take changes a whole lot more nuanced and deep-rooted than gun laws before Americans can put away the bulletproof vests.

PART FOUR

Shadows Fall

Going Viral

FIGHTING FOR OXYGEN IN TRUMP'S AMERICA

2020

Suddenly, the coronavirus pandemic has so upstaged and overshadowed what we will now remember as normal life that last month's anguish seems like trivial aggravation. In this genuine, once-in-a-lifetime national crisis, wouldn't it be comforting to have an elected leader as intelligent and mature as Barack Obama? Or even as intelligent and unreliably mature as Bill Clinton. Or even as capable of performing or simulating maturity as Ronald Reagan and G. W. Bush. Or even as intelligent, if perhaps twisted and corrupt, as Richard M. Nixon.

Instead, God help us, we have what we have, its face spray-painted the ocher color of old Spanish walls, its angry mouth puckered like a blowfish poised to swallow minnows. There's no doubt that its initial refusal to acknowledge the threat from this virus delayed our response and will result in the deaths of any number of American citizens. This is a grave charge, and I'm in accord with the journalists and Democrats who hope it might destroy the strange career of Donald Trump. But in all fairness, it may be too harsh to blame the whole metastasizing mess on one great fool in the White House. Remember that this is an old man (my age), notoriously stupid and no doubt cognitively challenged, who had been encouraged to believe that this year, 2020, would be his year of final triumph and vindication. He would be reelected and set up court in Mar-a-Lago as the true King of America, a destiny beyond his most addled dreams.

And then came Covid-19, a microscopic life form he couldn't see if it sat on his thumb, yet a thousand times more potent and more toxic than Donald Trump himself. Surrounded as he is by enabling sycophants and buffoons, is it any wonder that his first response to the pandemic was a fire wall of denial? As long as the federal government is our first line of defense against the virus, it's irresponsible to wish its representatives anything but

107

rapid success in the weeks to come. I'd sacrifice nearly anything to get rid of this terrible president—but probably not my life, or even my neighbor's.

It's true that he called the pandemic "a new hoax," as recently as February 28, and now says, "I felt it was a pandemic long before it was called a pandemic." His tiny brain is where all facts go to die. If he elects to "reopen" the nation prematurely against all the best medical advice, tens of thousands will die and history will remember him as the most lethal American psycho since Jim Jones spiked the Kool-Aid in Guyana. Yet far more important than pinning the blame on Trump, at least at this stage, is deciding how to proceed when and if this deadly microbe has finally lost its battle with our medical scientists. Once out of quarantine, where should America's weary survivors, creeping up out of their basements and root cellars, place their most urgent priorities? It would be a great relief to see Trump defeated in the November election, and to see Democrats regain control of the Senate. But neither of those victories would come close to curing the deeper sickness, this infection not viral but . . . systemic, spiritual? . . . that has served to place such power in the hands of reprehensible grifters like Donald Trump and Mitch McConnell.

Of course Joe Biden, somewhat past his prime, would make a much better, safer, saner president—though the only individuals who would not are in asylums and maximum security prisons. The sickness that preceded and may long outlast Covid-19 is one that will, unchecked, produce far worse things than one psychopathic realtor with a drowned orange mammal clutching his head. Trump's outrageous lies and venomous tweetstorms distract us from the rest of the Republican Party, where racism, xenophobia, and prehistoric stupidity are all epidemic. If you wanted to interview the most simpleminded public figure in the United States, this summer's Republican convention might be the first place to look. I even have a candidate. His name is Tommy Tuberville and he's famous, at least in Alabama, as a successful football coach at Auburn University.

Tuberville, a Republican candidate for one of Alabama's U.S. Senate seats, is a Christian who believes that Donald Trump was sent by God to save white people. Muslim terrorists control America's cities, he tells Alabama voters. "Sharia law has taken over," he said in March. "We have more Middle Easterners coming across that border at times than we do people from Latin America. They're coming over here to tear this country down." Really. And it's been over four decades since Coach Tuberville suffered his last concussion at the line of scrimmage. Another Southerner, evangelist Rick

Wiles of the TruNews website the White House has honored with press credentials, is offering his parishioners the same warning about Jews. The impeachment of Donald Trump was an attempted "Jew coup," according to Wiles. I assume he means Jewish Americans, since the far right tends to find common cause with Likudist Israelis.

Wiles commonly referred to Barack Obama as "a demon from hell." My home state of North Carolina can claim preacher/legislator Larry Pittman, one of the authors of the infamous "bathroom bill," who once equated Abraham Lincoln with Adolf Hitler. Another Tar Heel treasure is Christian Klan leader Christopher Barker, who became unhinged when the Spanish-language Univision network sent a Black Colombian reporter to interview him. On videotape, he called Ilia Calderón a "nigger" and threatened to kill her. The recent *New York Times* obituary for Barbara Harris, the first woman (and Black woman) ordained as an Episcopal bishop, quoted her response to the hate mail and death threats that followed her election: "Nobody can hate like Christians."

That's an arresting statement, one that appears to be true, and increasingly so in polarized, pandemic-haunted America. What do these rabid hatemongers have in common, besides professing Christianity? They're all white, they're all Republican, they all voted for Donald Trump, and they'll vote for him again. They're all part of "the base" that Hillary Clinton unwisely but accurately dubbed "the deplorables."

I'm hardly the kind of Christian who would ever proselytize, or vote to make Christianity a state religion. But there ought to be a way to take Christ back from false "Christians" who make a malignant mockery of the Gospels. In a Higher Court, their punishment for spreading hate and bearing false witness would be to listen to the Sermon on the Mount read by someone like Barbara Harris—hour after hour, for months on end.

For Tommy Tuberville and his like, it might not penetrate. But we have a much better chance of reclaiming Jesus than reclaiming the Republican Party. The recent deaths of two old-school Republican congressmen from upstate New York reminded me painfully of the dignity and decency that vanished when the GOP, executing Nixon's satanic "Southern strategy," reshaped itself as a white people's party anchored by the segregationist Dixiecrats of Strom Thurmond and Jesse Helms. Republicans who found racism repugnant were left behind, and only a few moderates continued to win elections on the Republican ticket. One of them was Amory Houghton, my mother's congressman in a rural district of western New York.

Houghton, who died at ninety-three in early March, was a wealthy, Harvard-educated aristocrat whose father and grandfather were both ambassadors. Prior to his nine terms in Congress he was the CEO of Corning Glass, a venerable international corporation founded by his family in 1851. He also supported civil rights, abortion rights, increases in the minimum wage, campaign-funding reforms, and an assault-weapon ban, and opposed the war in Iraq, Christian-mandated school prayer, and Bill Clinton's impeachment—all in defiance of his party's leadership. In his nineties he was a vocal critic of Donald Trump. Check, check, check. Everything you could ask from a thoughtful, progressive congressman, and entirely in line with the New York Republicanism that formed his philosophy. My father, a similar Republican, was scandalized by FDR's fiscal policies but would have cut off his own right hand before shaking Donald Trump's.

But the thing about Houghton that most endeared him to me was his personal response to letters from my mother. His were not the kind of letters from politicians you get today—usually emails begging for money—with your first name inserted at the top and all the rest canned. "Dear Dorothy," he would begin, and proceed to address each of the questions and concerns in her letter. And she would proudly show me her latest reply from "Amo," which is what everyone called him. My mother, a widowed, retired English teacher, was not a major contributor to Houghton's campaigns or a person with any influence outside her village of eight hundred souls.

Did he personally answer every constituent letter? How could he? But "Now that's a congressman!" is what I thought when I saw their correspondence. Once upon a time that was a Republican congressman. Another upstate Republican of the same stripe—and even more of a rebel liberal—was Richard Hanna of New York's Twenty-Second District, who died in March of cancer, at sixty-nine. Hanna, often alone on his side of the aisle, supported gay marriage, Planned Parenthood, and the Equal Rights Amendment. He despised Donald Trump so intensely ("a national embarrassment") that he bolted his party in 2016 and endorsed Hillary Clinton.

"I never left the Republican Party that I originally joined," Rep. Hanna told an interviewer. "I can only say that they've left me."

Under the celebrity birthday column in the local paper I was reading this morning, I found a relevant note: "On this day in 1854, the Republican Party was founded by abolitionists at a school in Wisconsin." That was the actual Republican Party, the party of Abraham Lincoln that somehow became the party of Donald Trump and Jim Crow. In reality only the name is the same.

The party's traditional fiscal caution devolved into ruthless contempt for the unfortunate and virtual piracy of the nation's wealth. Everything else Republican ancestors believed in—tolerance, equality, human rights, even free speech—is long gone from the party platform, traded away for racists' votes.

Party affiliation can become almost hereditary, and sometimes I'm not sure that these middle-class, educated Republicans, the country-club and Chamber of Commerce crowd, fully understand who they're sleeping with when they vote Republican in the twenty-first century. I try to give them the benefit of the doubt. But the USA, compromised at its very roots by slavery and Native American genocide, has always had a dark side. A very dark side, one that has required vigilant denial. John Adams—the abolitionist New England Founder, not one of the Southern slaveholding Founders—appreciated Shakespeare's *Othello* but wrote to a friend that Desdemona probably got what she deserved for sleeping with a Black man. Cringe? Then don't read the private letters of Adams's greatgrandson Henry Brooks Adams, one of the nineteenth century's most gifted and respected historians, whose impassioned anti-Semitism will curl your hair. In 1939, two years before Pearl Harbor, pro-Nazi Americans inspired by national icons Henry Ford and Charles Lindbergh held a rally in New York's Madison Square Garden. Twenty thousand native fascists attended, wildly cheering speeches that praised Hitler and warned of the "Jewish menace."

That dark side has always been there, but it's rarely so obvious who's feeding it and profiting from it. I've heard enough nonsense about the "populism" of the Right. The modern Republican Party is defined by bigotry and religious hypocrisy. It's a rank sty crowded with blind pigs, and what they're eating you don't want to step in. Since Trump joined the anti-Obama Birther cult, his personal racism has never been in doubt; hate crimes against all minorities have more than doubled since he was elected. On the alt-right color chart, white does not include Jews, Muslims, or Latin Americans. Roman Catholics (Sean Hannity?) were never white enough for the KKK, which once recruited Trump's father. If anything positive can come from a terrifying pandemic, a shared national ordeal, might it be a modest upsurge in altruism and fraternal feeling, a sense among lukewarm white Republicans and independents that not all politics are about us and "them"?

Is that too much to hope for, that a nation ravaged by a killer virus could relearn enough about compassion to recognize that the GOP has none?

Since 2016 it has been spinning toward the dark side, the black hole of fascism, at warp speed. To fuel your worst fears, keep your eye on Immigration and Customs Enforcement, which under Trump has adopted tactics the gestapo would have applauded.

This is not a recruiting poster for the Democrats, who at least half the time will break your heart. They occupy the moral high ground that was thrust upon them, rather than earned, when their Solid South defected to the enemy. A reduced but still solid South, Jim Crow's evil empire, is the concrete that holds Trump's baleful base together. A party defined by Donald Trump, Rush Limbaugh, "Bathroom Bill" Pittman, and Tommy Tuberville is no longer an option for people of ordinary good will and good sense. White nationalists have no place in the enlightened democracy the United States of America has sometimes aspired and always pretended to be. Either they fail or we all fail. If you survive the virus and find yourself still thinking Republican, think twice while your conscience still shows a pulse.

Darkness at Dawn

THE CAMPUS IN CRISIS

2018

A recent study of twenty thousand young adults, average age twenty, reported that 52 percent were experiencing hopelessness, 70 percent felt "very sad and lonely," and 37 percent were so depressed they could barely function. Sixty percent felt overwhelming anxiety, 38 percent felt overwhelming anger. Eleven percent had considered suicide and 1.3 percent—some 250 individuals—had actually attempted it. From this profile of a tortured Lost Generation, we imagine a sample from Third World countries like El Salvador, where young people driven from their villages by violence and starvation walk hundreds of miles toward "freedom" and end up in American concentration camps. Or young Afghans, whose families cooperated with the invading Americans, now awaiting Taliban retribution when the last Yankee regiment is gone. Syrians, maybe, refugees with their futures destroyed by that dreadful war at the nexus of all the world's anxiety.

If those were Americans in this survey, surely they were members of disadvantaged minorities, trapped in the violence and drug abuse of abandoned urban ghettoes. Or soon-to-be-dispersed kids from fading small towns, high school graduates and dropouts who know that the only jobs they'll ever find are hundreds of miles away in those frightening cities.

Those would be educated guesses. Guess again. The twenty thousand near adults in this study, conducted in 2017 by the American College Health Association, made up the undergraduate student body of the University of North Carolina at Chapel Hill. UNC-CH—alma mater of my daughter and my son-in-law, onetime employer of my wife, the pride of North Carolina's prideful university system, and one of the most venerable and prestigious public universities in the United States. This storied campus, this oasis of learning guarded for a century by the recently toppled statue of a Confederate soldier called Silent Sam—this epicenter of depression and misery?

These students, these tortured outpatients, are the cream of the crop. They include the most gifted, many of the most affluent and the most privileged in every respect. Twenty years ago their bright futures, and their faith in them, would have been taken for granted. If more than half of these elite undergraduates feel hopeless and nearly three-quarters are sad and lonely, we can only conclude—tentatively, since this is virgin territory for psychiatrists—that their less fortunate peers feel even worse. A whole generation consumed by anguish? And we're led to conclude that something new, something devastating and previously unexamined, is going terribly wrong.

Here's where I skate out onto thin ice. It doesn't take a reader much research—a quick Wikipedia check—to confirm that I'm a septuagenarian. I graduated from college during the Johnson administration. One pompous comparison between my generation and this one and we have an easily dismissed "Why, back in my day . . ." exercise like the ones I made fun of when I was at the other end of the age gap. It's too easy to dismiss these troubled undergraduates as pampered crybabies. College students today have plenty to worry about. It's July as I write this, and climate change is rendering the South, and lots of other places, virtually uninhabitable. Geopolitics are combustible. War, even nuclear war, is in the air, and the current president of the United States is a senile racist sex criminal with an ego the size of a bus and a brain the size of a walnut. White supremacy is coming back into style, the population bomb is ticking, defenders of the environment—our fragile planet—are overwhelmed by corporate predators and their captive politicians.

It's no picnic looking for a future, one often burdened by scandalous student debt, a specter few of us encountered fifty years ago. The financial inflation in higher education is the result of a vicious conspiracy between the lenders and the schools, and one of the best reasons to distrust or even despise the establishment. But the sixties, my friend, were no carefree stroll down Fraternity Row. Give us credit. There was a universal draft for a pointless, bloody war, there were friends and relatives coming home in body bags. A president was murdered while I was in college. Just who had him killed, and why, we'll probably never know. (If you still believe in the insane single shooter with no affiliations, you're at least incurious if not outright gullible.) In 1968 that president's brother was murdered, too, and so was Martin Luther King. There was Kent State and Selma, Alabama. Vietnam and civil rights polarized Americans almost as radically as they're polarized today, over our repulsive president and his racially feral Republican Party.

We had our issues. But do I in any way suspect—I was never considered a happy camper, myself—that deep down half of us felt hopeless and two out of five were too distressed to function? Come on. We were twenty, for Christ's sake. There were so many places we hadn't seen, books we hadn't read, flavors we hadn't tasted, women we hadn't met. (I speak purely from a male point of view on that, but didn't women have similar high hopes?) There was all of life ahead, however it might turn out, and much of it looked damned inviting at the outset. And yes, we were the privileged ones, too.

I had one college friend who was determined to commit suicide, and he succeeded on his third try. He even preached hopelessness and suicide, over beer in fraternity basements. I liked Bill and considered him brilliant, but his fatal argument was unconvincing. I thought he was mentally ill; I think most of his friends agreed with me. (Another classmate attempted suicide, but he chose to hang himself from a pipe that bent a little under his weight. He was 6'4", luckily, and when his toes touched the rug he lacked the suicidal will to lift them and strangle. After serving some hospital time, this classmate became a respected businessman and citizen. But he was known to us by the nickname "Too Tall.")

On campus today, would suicidal Bill be a leader and a prophet, instead of a tragic outlier? Would his determination to destroy himself win him disciples, instead of friends like us who shook our heads when we talked about him, and schemed to distract him from his deadly purpose? Something profound has changed when so many young people, given exclusive opportunities to prosper in one of the world's wealthiest countries, see only gloom and sorrow on the road ahead.

A lot of things have changed in fifty years, including the reputation of America, once a role model among nations, now more feared and psychoanalyzed than admired. Perceptive people around the globe see us set on a collision course with some of our worst instincts. Who, in the summer of 2019, could argue with that? But the national trajectory is not one of the prime concerns of depressed sophomores. Every survey indicates that their anxiety is infinitely more personal than global. So the question becomes, "What is the most dramatic, what is the defining difference between growing up in the sixties and growing up in the twenty-first century?"

It's no mystery. These students are the first Americans born and entirely marinated in the age of digital communication, the age of the internet and the "devices" that enable it—most notoriously the cell phone—and of the metastasizing phenomenon of social media. Sven Birkerts, in his prophetic book *The Gutenberg Elegies*, described their life, now the life of the majority of Americans, as "hive life." Its consequence, an interconnectedness so complete that privacy becomes a quaint memory, seemed so toxic to Birkerts that his final advice to his readers was "Reject it." This was in 1994, at the dawn of the technological revolution and the promiscuous sharing that transformed every society and left Birkerts sounding like a voice from the Middle Ages.

To those of us who remember the way it was before, the difference feels vast, intergalactic. A cousin of mine in her teens looked at me suspiciously, as if I might be lying to her, when I admitted that I never made phone calls when I was her age. Cells hadn't been invented; parents discouraged us from using their home phones to call friends. After a long day of school and sports practices most of us were relieved to be alone or with our families in the evening. Weekends we met in the park, on the ball field or the basketball courts. Hardly ever by prearrangement, either.

Whatever we were deprived of, we didn't know it or miss it. Who knew that most human beings, and especially younger ones, had been yearning for the technology to unburden themselves of their ill-informed opinions and intimate secrets—all for rapt audiences of voyeurs and exhibitionists like themselves? If life before "hive life" sounds profoundly weird to young people today, take it from me that "trolls," "Twitter mobs," "cyberbullying," and armies of virtual "friends" and "followers" would have sounded like freaky science fiction to the kids we were back then.

They still seem very strange, to me. It took me longer to grasp the addictive power of these gadgets and networks because I seem mercifully immune to their charms. David Brooks of *The New York Times* describes the social mediasphere as "a competitive, volatile attention economy"—the coin of this realm is attention. Attention, the raw material of celebrity, is not for everyone. It may be a seductive goal when you're twenty, but only a hollow freak like Donald Trump still feeds on it at fifty. I was probably lucky, when I was very young, to work a job that involved a lot of professional contact with celebrities. The smart ones never denied the economic or sexual advantages of celebrity, but they were nearly all sick to death of the attention.

"Attention and affection have gone from being private bonds to being publicly traded goods," writes Brooks, expanding his argument. "People ensconced in social media are more likely to be on perpetual alert: How are my ratings at this moment? If you orient your life around attention, you will always feel slighted. You will always feel emotionally unsafe."

The hyperearnest but eloquent Brooks is on to something here, something that may help us understand an epidemic of unhappy undergraduates. Has hive life become a life of perpetual performance, with every effort ranked and reviewed? Wouldn't this obliterate a fragile ego, and chip away relentlessly at a strong one? But Brooks and I are only journalists, laypersons with no special knowledge of the brain's pathways or their influence on human behavior. A more authoritative observer is the late Oliver Sacks, neurologist and bestselling author, who sounded an alarm in a *New Yorker* essay that was published shortly before he died.

"A majority of the population is now glued almost without pause to phones or other devices—jabbering, texting, playing games, turning more and more to virtual reality of every sort," Sacks lamented. "Everything is public now, potentially; one's thoughts, one's photos, one's movements, one's purchases. There is no privacy and apparently little desire for it in a world devoted to non-stop use of social media.... Those trapped in this virtual world are never alone, never able to concentrate and appreciate in their own way, silently."

In "our bewitched, besotted society," Sacks continued, "younger people who have grown up in our social media era have no personal memory of how things were before, and no immunity to the seductions of digital life. What we are seeing—and bringing on ourselves—resembles a neurological catastrophe on a gigantic scale."

"A neurological catastrophe." Strong words, which carry greater weight because they were his critical parting shot, possibly the last words Sacks wrote. He was horrified by the spectacle of adults who seemed mesmerized by cell phones, but his is not essentially a Luddite argument—though I think Sacks, Brooks, and I, along with the prophet Birkerts, would all be proud to accept the "Luddite" label that has become such a pejorative in digital society. I don't deny that I once dismissed Silicon Valley's contribution to modern America as "a thousand solutions for which there were no problems." But any fair critic will admit that digital technology offered positive changes in our basic communications. I embraced email because, like H. L. Mencken when it was an electronic miracle, I always hated the telephone. It enabled people to seize my attention when they were not welcome to it, and it was a time consumer no polite person could control.

Sacks's core argument is biological, and behavioral. It's about the addiction, the powerful grip on the user that no engineer in microchip land could have anticipated, though no doubt it delighted his employers. Remember when the BlackBerry was the trendy smartphone, and enslaved users dubbed it the "CrackBerry"? Nearly every addictive agent offers real benefits to the addict. I understand that tobacco products delivered meaningful relief to generations of nervous and neurotic individuals. At the same time, unfortunately, their cigarettes were killing them in at least fifty different ways.

This is the way the digital revolution will be judged by history, and the judgment may be coming sooner than we think. Social media—in essence, communicating more unnecessary things to more unnecessary people, more efficiently—will most likely be the first target of the counterrevolution. It is out of control. It's not just the extreme pathology the "attention economy" has begun to provoke: the college "boys" who gang-raped an unconscious coed and "posted" the video on their favorite platform, or the lunatic in Utica, New York, who slashed his seventeen-year-old date's throat, nearly decapitating her, and then posted snapshots of her corpse on Instagram and Snapchat. The criminals' impulse to share these atrocities is almost as frightening as the atrocities themselves. But the main threat to our collective sanity and survival, already provoking anxious reactions from parents all across the country, is the pandemic of screen addiction among children many years younger than college students.

Screen-time consultants, parenting coaches offering what they describe as "digital detox," are prospering, charging up to $250 an hour for their services. Some of their recommendations are as simplistic as getting your kids a dog or a cat, or buying them a ball and teaching them to throw it or kick it. In Austin, Texas, and Concord, Massachusetts, parents' groups have been organized around pledges to deny their children smartphones until they're in the eighth grade at least. "Movement" is the key, according to one consultant—these innocent victims need to be reminded that they have bodies as well as fingers and thumbs. (Epidemic obesity seems to be another side effect of the digital revolution.) YouTube, Instagram, and the video game called Fortnite have been targeted as especially addictive distractions.

A kind of panic has set in, at least among relatively aware parents who aren't helpless digital addicts themselves. Many of them realize that they're the first parents in history who have to fight for their children's souls, or at least their attention, against this whole seductive wired world, this buzzing superhive of amoral activity with an agenda that's essentially commercial. These parents may be the main source of hope, and look what's stacked against them. Trillions have been earned by the people who conceived the digital smorgasbord, and they'll spend many billions to maintain and expand it. Politicians, many of them purchased by media moguls out of petty cash, will not be a useful counterforce. A powerful, responsible news source like *The New York Times* may publish David Brooks's neo-Luddite musings on the evils of the attention economy, but just over the page there are articles on "Snapchat celebrities," "TikTok stars," and the potency of social media "influencers" written without any irony that I can detect.

There's no proven connection between screen-addicted sixth graders and suicidal college sophomores, no available studies that trace individuals' lives from their first cell phones and video games to their first attempt to overdose. But the data is there about their widespread misery at an age when most of us old-timers—the similarly lucky ones—felt undeservedly blessed. There's a reason to be found somewhere, and you may be holding it in your hand.

No one is less qualified than I am to examine the digital experience from the inside, from the personal insights of a cybertraveler. Few are less qualified to tell undergraduates to let go and cheer up. My sophomore roommate nicknamed me "MOCS" or "Emmo" for short, for my frequent moaning renditions of my favorite folk song, "Man of Constant Sorrow." Beckett and Dostoyevsky were the first writers I couldn't stop reading, Schopenhauer and Nietzsche were my philosophers of choice. Back when I had academic ambitions, I committed myself to the majestic melancholy of Thomas Hardy. The irony isn't lost on me.

The world I grew up in is dead and gone, and it won't be resurrected. The trick is not to turn back the clock, but to look ahead with our eyes wide open. Hive life may be here, but does it deserve to be here to stay? If it seemed to be making young people happier and more productive, I'd say, "God bless you, then," and retreat to the museum where I belong. Instead we read that 40 percent are too soul-sick to function, and that triage appointments for our university's psychiatric services have more than doubled since 2013. Please consider the possibility that we may be on the wrong track, and proceeding at a reckless speed.

"The Gates of Hell"—
Swinging Wide?

2021

The world is a strange place and in it lie things of another
nature, a bent order, and beyond a certain point
there are no rules to make men mind.
—LARRY BROWN, "A Roadside Resurrection"

As the dismal summer of 2021 staggered toward its woeful conclusion, "the worst of times" seemed hard upon us, and the only
relevant question was "Can it get much worse?" After the tragic
Second Coming of the coronavirus, those surging body counts and hard-
pressed hospitals, the vaccine wars, hurricanes and floods and wildfires,
the painful conclusion of the Afghanistan fiasco, primitive legislative assaults on our voting and reproductive rights—how much worse could it get,
here in our once-free, once-favored USA? The answer, trust me, is "very
much worse." Some broad hints: You could balance a shot glass on its lacquered orange forelock, its tailor apprenticed with Barnum and Bailey, and
it was never caught telling the truth unless you asked it if it was still hungry. There's a hungry, attention-starved thing out there that could make the
summer of 2021 look like a morning stroll through sunlit meadows.

That second Second Coming, the Restoration of Donald J. Trump, is a
cause so weird and suicidal that foreign observers, friend and foe alike, fail
to believe that it's still thriving in America. The far right's pitiful convul-
sion in Washington September 18 was such a flaccid nonevent that never-
Trumpers were encouraged to believe that the ex-president and his Stop-
the-Steal fantasies of returning to office have lost momentum. My guess is
that the impotent, sparsely attended rally in support of the January 6 insurrectionists simply showed us the difference between a police force that
couldn't imagine the stupidity and ferocity of the Trump alt-right, and one

that's now well prepared for it. January 6 was a lesson that won't have to be learned again.

If only the general population could learn its lessons as well as the Capitol police. Now as then, in 2016 and 2020, the unanswerable question is not "How could so many millions of voters be fooled by this fool?" but "How could anyone?" New books on the Trump presidency, notably *Peril* from Bob Woodward and Robert Costa, portray a president so erratic, hysterical, and profane that no satirist could do him justice. I've worked in a steel mill and in major league locker rooms where the f-word is heard less often than it was uttered in the Oval Office. One of Trump's charms for a certain class of voter is that he's a man who's had every advantage but behaves like men who had none. And now these books make it clear that virtually everyone who worked with or against him knew that he was insane.

"Who knows what he might do?" Speaker Nancy Pelosi asked General Mark Milley, chairman of the Joint Chiefs of Staff. "He's crazy. You know he's crazy. He's been crazy for a long time. So don't say you don't know what his state of mind is."

"Madam Speaker," General Milley replied, "I agree with you on everything." The most frightening revelation in the Woodward/Costa book is that Milley was so alarmed by Trump's postelection derangement that he went outside diplomatic channels to contact a Chinese general—to reassure him that Trump wouldn't bomb China to distract the world from his defeat. For what appears to have been a heroic effort to save the human race from nuclear annihilation, Milley has now been branded a traitor by most Republicans. *Peril* also reveals that Attorney General William Barr mocked Rudy Giuliani and Trump's wild team of defeat deniers, which Barr referred to as "the clown car." America survived—more or less—an administration with its top military official and its top legal official in agreement that their boss was a ridiculous lunatic.

But polls still show that 60 percent of Republican voters admire Donald Trump and would choose him again in 2024. Trump's immunity, his lifetime free pass from truth and responsibility, is an infuriating conundrum with only one explanation I can comprehend. An explanation that links it, if I'm right, to the most pressing of America's current agonies, the only one it can—and must—address immediately and forcefully.

News item: President Biden issues a broad and entirely necessary vaccine mandate. The idiot governor of South Carolina, one Henry McMaster, declares that he will fight the president and the mandate "to the gates of Hell."

The governor of Alabama, a state where every ICU bed is occupied and Covid-sick patients are stretched out in waiting rooms, calls Biden's mandates "outrageous, overreaching."

Besides stretching the outer limits of demagoguery and reminding us that Republicans have no Biden policy besides total obstruction, what can we say is happening here? Vaccine refusal is something that cannot be tolerated. Public health has nothing to do with "freedom" or individual rights. Citizenship always entails certain risks and sacrifices, and compromises for the common good. Consider only military service, and the military draft. These doctors who want to vaccinate you are one hundred times more competent, and more concerned with your personal welfare, than the people who sent you to Vietnam or Afghanistan. Your refusal to be vaccinated, like a refusal to fire back when your company is under attack, might cost you your own life. But in the chain of consequences it will certainly cause the deaths of many others.

Most of us dislike mandates. I have my own libertarian streak, a "Tell me I must and I swear that I won't" streak that's plagued me since grammar school. But there is no rational argument for refusing the Covid vaccine, any more than there's a rational argument for embracing and reinstating Donald Trump. So where does this organized, stubborn resistance to proven vaccines—infecting a quarter of America's population and more than half the population of several states—draw its fuel and its inexhaustible supply of falsehoods?

Look hard at the media, at an information culture in crisis. News outlets and websites that feature bald-faced, preposterous, dangerous lies—the presidential election was stolen, the Covid-19 pandemic was a hoax, climate change is a hoax, the sacking of the Capitol last January 6 was "a normal tourist visit," Nazi demonstrators are antifa agents in disguise, Democrats are Satanists and pedophiles, etc.—continue to prosper and proliferate. Social media extends and intensifies their poisonous reach. A recent *Wall Street Journal* series on Facebook and its notorious algorithm quotes the company's own researchers on the perils of giving the information customers just what they want. "Publishers and political parties were reorienting their posts toward outrage and sensationalism," internal memos complained. "Our approach has had unhealthy side effects on important slices of public content, such as politics and news. This is an increasing liability. Misinformation, toxicity and violent content are inordinately prevalent among reshares."

"I fall heavily on the side of trusting science more than something you read on Facebook," actor Matt Damon offered, helpfully, but few starstruck anti-vaxxers were lining up behind him. It's not news that the American Right openly despises facts, dismisses science, and ridicules expertise, or that extremist news sources and their social media bullhorns have substantially undermined public trust in our institutions. Polls show that trust in the medical establishment has slipped from 75 percent to 25 percent since the 1970s, and trust in higher education has dropped nine percentage points in just three years, to below 50 percent. Trust in the free press may never recover from Donald Trump. This war on truth—on individual, uncomfortable truths and on Truth as an essential civic guidepost—has been the foundation of every dictatorship, every authoritarian government. H. L. Mencken, a harsh critic of American democracy, warned us one hundred years ago that working democracy depends entirely on an educated electorate and reliable sources of information. He was not impressed with the way it was going in 1921. What if the sacred majority is ignorant, loves its ignorance, and is essentially unteachable? Mencken asked, at his most alarmed. What happens to the reasonable, the responsible, and the well-meaning who try to live among them? What then? Mencken, of course, could never have imagined Twitter and Facebook—or even Fox News.

With so many sources peddling deliberate audience-tested and -targeted misinformation, it's getting much harder to maintain the critical learning curve that sustains a democracy. And a sad thing we've learned from the Trump cult and the anti-vaccine movement is that their believers don't randomly choose fantasy and disinformation from a confusingly vast menu of news choices. It's *all* they eat. The vaccine war, for example, is not a real quarrel between liberals and conservatives. Little ideology is involved. It's simply, starkly a quarrel between people who earnestly pursue the truth about the world they live in, and other people who inhabit and cling to alternate realities, where facts are not honored or even welcome. They live in self-serving, self-protecting antireality chambers they construct out of inherited prejudice, wishful thinking, and the mediasphere's cheapest materials.

We don't need Mencken to remind us that the unteachables have always been with us. And we've always been cursed with cynics who sell poisonous snake oil to the simpleminded. But in the past they had nothing like the internet and its social media echo chambers to capture, program, and control the weakest minds and wills. We recognize and to some extent pity the simple, even as they doom themselves and others. But what about the cynics, the opportunists who advance and enrich themselves on the gullibility of the uninformed? Check the educational backgrounds of Republicans like Senator Ted Cruz of Texas and Governor Ron DeSantis of Florida, and you might be surprised to find the names of some of America's most prestigious universities. These people are all vaccinated; they all know perfectly well that Donald Trump is crazy and that most of his passionate supporters are mouth breathers and knuckle draggers.

Their hypocrisy is infernal, possibly unprecedented. And what about media frauds like Tucker Carlson and Mark R. Levin (whose books were recently ranked first and second on the *New York Times*' nonfiction bestseller charts)? Carlson was a wealthy boy who went to an upscale college. He was even a working journalist at one time. Does he really believe any of the things he says, the outrageous things that have made him famous and wealthy? I'm an elderly gentleman who hasn't won a fight since the sixth grade, but if Tucker Carlson ever walked into a room where I could reach him, he would need bodyguards to escape unharmed. There is no place in hell hot enough for hypocrites like Carlson or DeSantis. When Governor Henry McMaster makes his last stand on the vaccine mandate down at the gates of hell, he'll find a lot of familiar faces waiting in line.

Wired America's most dubious twenty-first-century achievement is a deadly nuclear core of ferocious ignorance—or ignorant ferociousness—that cynical demagogues like Carlson, DeSantis, and Texas Governor Greg Abbott manipulate ruthlessly, in the service of nothing more worthy than their own egos and careers. This deadly core is indifferent and prejudicial to the general welfare, to the health of the nation. They're traitors and public enemies without meaning to be, so profound is their ignorance. They're possible in this time, in our time, as in no time that came before us.

Dark Clouds Gathering

HOMEGROWN FASCISTS SHOW THEIR TEETH

2021

One by one in recent years, objections to describing
militant Trumpism as fascist have fallen away.
—JEFF SHARLET, *The Undertow*

A few years ago I was empaneled at Duke University with a formidable pair of writers, the Romanian poet Andrei Codrescu, who was then teaching at LSU, and the Chilean novelist/playwright Ariel Dorfman, a Duke professor. I'm embarrassed to admit that I no longer remember who sponsored this event or exactly what we were attempting to resolve. I know we discussed politics and geopolitics. Dorfman and Codrescu owed some of their political gravitas, of course, to the long shadows of the dictators who had seized their native countries. Dorfman had written eloquently about the bloody Pinochet years in Chile, and Codrescu's history with the Ceauşescu regime in Romania had made him NPR's resident critic of authoritarian government.

I remember joking that my own defense of democracy was limited to my disparagement of North Carolina's Neanderthal senator Jesse Helms, a relatively harmless old ogre compared to their jackboot dictators. At the time I think we all agreed that nothing quite as frightening as Pinochet or Ceauşescu could ever happen in a mature democracy like America's.

I'm no longer confident of that, and it's no longer a joking matter. For years everyone positioned to the left of center prudently avoided the word "fascist" and comparisons to Nazi Germany when the latest Republican outrage reduced us to tears. One loaded word, when everyone hears it, can have serious consequences in politics. The conventional wisdom is that Hillary Clinton damaged her campaign in 2016 when she referred to the Trump base as "deplorables." This was supposed to be an instance of a pedigreed Wellesley/Yale graduate's sneering condescension to less educated and less fortunate Americans. But we're no longer in doubt about which "deplorables" she actually had in mind—we saw them storming the U.S. Capitol on January 6, 2021, spurred on by an orange-faced baboon who still refers to January 6 as "a beautiful day."

Avoiding words like "Hitler" and "Nazi" was rhetorically wise and showed admirable restraint, while Trump and his far-right chorus line held a monopoly on reckless exaggeration and hate-triggering name calling. An odd thing I've learned in a half-century of public discourse is that the very worst people invariably accuse their antagonists of the things of which they themselves are most guilty. When they call you a thief or a liar or a pedophile, you can be almost certain that they're lying and stealing, or worse. Listen carefully to Donald Trump if you think I'm wrong. In his Mother's Day message he calls Democrats "fascists" and "lunatics."

We stomached the contempt for the rule of law and for most norms and precedents, we recoiled from the mindless, belligerent patriotism that anchors every right-wing movement (how is "MAGA" so different from "Deutschland Über Alles"?). We saw swastikas in Charlottesville and on the steps of the Capitol, and still most responsible voices on the Left held their fire, avoiding historical references to Kristallnacht and the Beer Hall Putsch.

But now I see that this era of well-bred, dignified progressive restraint is coming to an end. The Republicans' fiercest and most reliable critics have begun to take their gloves off. The former Labor Secretary Robert Reich, writing in *The Progressive Populist*, offered a stark but in no sense excessive warning: "The Republican Party is no longer committed to democracy. It is rapidly becoming the American fascist party." Picking up Reich's challenge, Thom Hartmann cut right to the chase, the inevitable comparison between Germany in 1933 and America ninety years later. "The parallels to today's America are startling," Hartmann writes. He goes on to list and explain them—the racism, anti-Semitism, and homophobia, the book bans, the captive party media, the censorship of school curricula, the contempt for artists and intellectuals. But Hartmann's most important point—familiar to journalists but unclear to most Americans—is that the current Republican Party, like the National Socialist Party, is an unlikely but lethally potent coalition of the most cynical plutocrats and a furious, gullible underclass eager to scapegoat minorities for its failures.

Even Hitler, we learn, had his friendly billionaires. And Donald Trump's claim that he's the champion ("I am your warrior," no less) of America's struggling underdog is right out of Hitler's playbook, right out of *Mein Kampf*. So are Trump's apocalyptic warnings, varying only from "Our country is dying" to "Our country is dead." Then and now, demagogues' soundtracks are interchangeable. It's highly unlikely that a reelected President Trump would be loading Jews and homosexuals into boxcars. Didn't his daughter convert to Judaism? But the threat of mob violence like the kind that exploded in Washington on January 6 was a key to the intimidation of "good Germans" in the 1930s, and when Trump said the goons who sacked the Capitol "were there with love in their hearts" I was nearly driven to violence myself.

The parallels are ample and disturbing. But one great difference between Germany in the 1930s and America today—and between America and any nation, at any time—is our frightening distribution of firearms among civilians. Any non-American who reads that there are more than 400 million guns in a nation of 330 million people is struck speechless. Add that one-third of our citizens own all of them and you realize you're staring at an armed paranoid minority that could start a world war of its own. Little wonder, really, that we've suffered more than two hundred mass shootings in the first four months of 2023. "I'm sticking close to home these days because, right now, humanity scares me," Brian Broome wrote in *The Washington Post*. "This country scares me."

Me too, buddy. Maybe the most horrible consequence of the arming of America is that the irrational paranoia anchoring our gun cult is becoming rational fear, for many people in many places. When every driver on the highway may be locked and loaded and every pedestrian packing, human nature guarantees a regular diet of mayhem. Of course not all of these concealed-carry lunatics are MAGA Republicans. Well, not all of them. But the state legislatures that are trying to *ease* restrictions on gun ownership in the face of these constant massacres—I'm ashamed to admit that North Carolina's legislature is one of them—are all red state and Republican controlled. President Biden's crusade to ban assault rifles, a minor concession to sanity, is being blocked by the NRA-owned-and-emasculated Republicans who control the House of Representatives.

A wide selection of Republican candidates have had themselves photographed flaunting their AR-15s, including congresswomen Lauren Boebert of Colorado and Georgia's wild-eyed war mom Marjorie Taylor Greene (who said something like "We don't hunt animals, we hunt tyrants."???). In the neofascist era we're entering, there's nothing in the political ecosystem more frightening than Republican women.

GOP Nazis didn't invent the gun cult or motiveless mass shootings, which have evolved from a deep, dark place in the American psyche. The novelist Paul Auster has published a new book, *Bloodbath Nation*, which traces this pathology all the way back to the Indian wars and attempts to answer the simple question "What makes us the most violent country in the Western world?" But there's no question that the NRA and its captive legislators, no less than the storm troopers who call themselves things like Oath Keepers and Proud Boys, are a big part of the MAGA juggernaut and the looming fascist threat. Gun violence has already turned the USA into an undesirable destination, with Amnesty International warning foreign travelers to "exercise caution" within our borders. Trump's reelection—or even his failure and refusal to accept it—might unleash unprecedented chaos.

We no longer have a safe place to hide from armed fanatics. Even a Democratic sweep of the White House and both houses of Congress would barely cool the fascist fever that seems to be burning in the Heartland. Journalist Jeff Sharlet, who specializes in exposing the hypocrisy of MAGA Christians, has just published *The Undertow*, which represents years of face-to-face conversations with Americans who have voted, and will vote, for Trump. His reports from the field are bone-chilling. His subjects, according to Joseph O'Neill's review in *The New York Times*, "reveal themselves in their full intransigence, menace and delusional mindset." Sharlet leaves the scene feeling more shaken up and pessimistic than ever. QAnon craziness and the widespread belief that the Clintons are child-eating pedophiles didn't shake the reporter as much as the militias and the obvious preparation for violence. Sharlet concluded that what he was witnessing was "the undertow of civil war."

The GOP has lurched so far to the Right that any Republican president will represent a body blow to democracy. Donald Trump is not the founder or even the linchpin of the American neofascist movement. He's more like the famous face on the cereal box. But he is a special case. Here's a man who was elected president with no experience or even knowledge of government, a fool who thought he'd been crowned King of America and performed as expected, like Ubu Roi. Stupid, ignorant, amoral, and now indisputably demented, he's back on the campaign trail, a clown with a spray-painted face, a yard-long necktie, and a slapstick act that's an insult to the political process. "Unhinged" is the word used most often by people who've experienced him close-up. He's been indicted for financial crimes by a grand jury, and found liable for sexual assault by a civil jury in New York. Does that mean he'll have to register as a sex offender in Florida? Will his Mar-a-Lago neighbors protest that he's dragging down the neighborhood?

This sad act should be playing to empty houses everywhere. To a reasonable person, it seems impossible that any voter, even one, would still consider Donald Trump presidential material. Yet here's a headline that reads "Biden's Approval Numbers Are Bleak," over a story that shows Trump leading both Biden and his Republican rival Ron DeSantis in the latest polls. A post-indictment poll indicated that 70 percent of the Republican Party was sticking with Trump. Many of those voters complained that Joe Biden is too old to be president. Of course he is, and so is Trump, and so am I. But Biden sure looks a lot healthier than Doughboy Donald. And 90 percent of what he says makes sense and passes fact-checking, while 100 percent of Trump's outbursts fail both tests. I see Joe Biden as the Dutch boy with his finger in the dike that holds back the fascists—a hero, in my opinion.

Trump remains an enigma. People exploit him for their own purposes, but no one likes him or even struggles to understand him. None of the principal strains of American fascism explain his haunting career—not the bigotry he embraces, the harsh authoritarianism he admires, or the violence he flirts with. He is a one-off. He's the chief beneficiary of the willful blindness, uniquely American, that terrified Jeff Sharlet. Trump's adherents, in their astonishing numbers, seem to be people who resist reality, who don't want to think. What they want is to believe. Trumpism stands outside political calculations—his converts are the kind of people who fall prey to suicide cults, to religious charlatans, to false messiahs. They're ready to drink the Kool-Aid.

Remember Marshall Applewhite of the Heaven's Gate cult, Jim Jones in Jonestown, David Koresh and the Branch Davidians in Waco? They were megalomaniacs, messianic narcissists who painted on the large canvas and never betrayed the slightest doubt. Their true believers followed them to the grave. Americans who follow Donald Trump to the end of the line aren't going to fare much better, believe me. We can only pray that they don't take the rest of us with them.

.

PART FIVE

It's Twilight Time

Dante on Broadway

2018

One of New York City's most neglected historical landmarks is a tiny park almost directly across Columbus Avenue from Lincoln Center, the cultural mecca where multitudes of New Yorkers satisfy their passions for opera, dance, theater, jazz, or classical music. Situated at Sixty-Third Street where Broadway crosses Columbus and bends to the east, the park is a perfect triangle that measures one-seventh of an acre of Manhattan's precious real estate. Though I lived in the city for over a decade, attended many Lincoln Center performances, and once rented an apartment just thirty blocks up Broadway—though I've visited Manhattan hundreds of times since I moved to the provinces—I never noticed the park or the statue that graces it until last spring. How many times had I passed it in a taxicab, passed deep beneath it in a subway car, or even walked within sight of it, never registering that tall figure on the pedestal, standing there among the trees?

New York City guidebooks describe the park as an overlooked, all-but-forgotten curiosity, and mention the trees that obscure the statue with their branches, even when you're almost in its shadow. Even if you were staying at the Empire Hotel, with its front entrance a few yards across Sixty-Third Street from the park, you might miss it if you were in a hurry. I had never stayed at the Empire before this visit in May; since I was in no hurry one morning, I sat down at a little iron table at the edge of the park, with my Starbucks coffee and *The New York Times*—and looked up.

Which heroes of the past do we expect to see honored by urban statues? In the South, mostly generals. Everywhere, politicians, saints, philanthropists, famous athletes. I couldn't see the statue's head, up there among the spring leaves, but the larger-than-life-size (nine and a half feet, actually) male figure was dressed in an outfit that looked nothing like a military uniform, more like an academic gown or a priest's cassock that covered the big fellow down to his shoes. A medieval aristocrat's everyday streetwear, as it turned out, specifically Italian, Florentine, thirteenth century. If I had been sitting on the other side of the little park, I would have seen its name on a large iron sign: Dante Park.

Dante Alighieri. I wouldn't have been more surprised if I'd found a statue of Joan Rivers. Dante, prince of poets, author of *The Divine Comedy*, first bright beacon of the Italian Renaissance that ended Europe's Dark Ages. How did his graven image come to its perch above Broadway, and how long has it been staring north past Lincoln Center?

Since 1921, I discovered, since decades before Lincoln Center was developed, since a time when many of New York's cabs were still drawn by horses. For nearly a century Dante's statue has struck its attitude of lonely contemplation above one of the city's busiest thoroughfares. Dante Park was part of the generous vision of one remarkable immigrant, Carlo Barsotti (1850–1927), banker and publisher of the Italian-language newspaper *Il Progreso Italo-Americano*. Barsotti's fundraising talent and passion for his native Italy were largely responsible for Dante and for statues of at least three other Italian heroes—Columbus, Garibaldi, and the composer Giuseppe Verdi—that still stand watch in Manhattan today. A much larger statue of the poet—one account says it was fifty-nine feet tall—was commissioned by Barsotti from the same sculptor, Ettore Ximenes, and delivered in 1915. But the city fathers rejected it as too grandiose, and it was last seen gathering cobwebs in a warehouse in Hoboken, New Jersey.

I had barely made Dante's acquaintance and noted that his head, way up there in the branches, wore a crown of laurels, when my attention was deflected to a white panel truck that had stopped for a red light at Sixty-Third Street. In very large letters on its side panel, legible from a block away, was the name and nature of the owner's business:

"PROSHRED
Information Destruction at Your Door
Onsite Paper and Hard Drive Destruction

I'm serious. Look up Proshred online. Call me a slave to irony, a pushover for symbolism—I'm a relic of college English departments and graduate schools before Big Theory reared its ugly head. But with peripheral vision I could actually see Dante and the truck in the same visual frame, poet on the left, Proshred on the right, an ironic juxtaposition so jarring I could have spit up my coffee. Representing the thirteenth century, Dante, father of the modern Italian language, progenitor of the Renaissance, disciple of

Aristotle, a great poet whose sacred mission was to preserve the wisdom and literature of the ancient Greeks and Romans and protect their precious, fragile links to his own time and culture. Representing the twenty-first century, "Information Destruction at Your Door." Irony doesn't hit us much harder than that. I like to think that a lot of people, if they had shared my vision at that moment, would have been as blindsided as I was. Realistically, I know that 95 percent of the people who pass through Dante Park have never heard of the poet ("Dante? A wide receiver for the Browns?") and would have no negative response to a Proshred truck. And that, of course, is a huge percentage of the problem.

Dante and the great Italian writers who immediately followed him—Boccaccio, Petrarch—were devoted above all to continuity, the spinal cord of civilization. They were committed to saving and illuminating everything they judged profound, essential, and eloquent among the contributions of previous generations and previous civilizations. "Illumination" is the key word, the password of the Renaissance—shedding light. Setting aside the actual physical destruction of printed and digital information, the Proshred Final Solution, isn't it clear that the twenty-first century, awash and adrift in technology, is veering in the opposite direction? Whose hand is it on the dimmer switch, who benefits when we obscure, neglect, and trivialize the accumulated knowledge of the past and its printed artifacts?

In America's social media century, with an illiterate, Twitter-addicted liar steering the ship of state, even yesterday—the past twenty-four hours and their printed, taped, and digitalized record—is routinely erased, distorted, denied. There are idiots afoot who must start every day like the first day of creation, as empty of memory as Adam waking up in the Garden of Eden. In *The Divine Comedy*, Dante locates the shade of Aristotle, his philosophical idol, in Hell—he was a pagan, sorry—but honors him with the august title "Master of those who know." What can we make of a country where the flow of information is dominated by the "Master of those who know nothing"?

"As a society, we have somehow fallen into a collective amnesia in thinking that it doesn't matter when the highest officeholder in the land doesn't tell the truth," wrote Mark Sanford, the Republican congressman from South Carolina who lost his reelection primary because he refused to kiss the stumpy ring finger of Donald Trump. The philosopher Hannah Arendt, a Jew who fled Nazi Germany after she was jailed by the gestapo, wrote about the degradation of language and information in a fascist society: "In an everchanging, incomprehensible world the masses had reached the point where they would, at the same time, believe everything and nothing, think that everything was possible and that nothing was true."

The political implications of cultural amnesia are frightening enough. We elected a president who dismisses every unwelcome fact as "fake news" and tells his supporters, "What you're seeing and what you're reading is not what's happening." He's not merely implying, he's declaring unequivocally that any information he hasn't supplied or sanctioned is worthless. And if you buy that, you might enjoy making Russia, Turkey, Syria, or the Philippines your homeland. You have no business in the United States, where a free and obstreperous press is a priceless legacy and our only real insurance against tyranny.

But the political crisis may not be the most depressing aspect of America's decline. Electoral politics can turn on a dime, as we learned in 2016. There may yet be someone sane and competent at the wheel, before chaos engulfs us. Maybe even someone honest. What disturbs me even more is my sense of a culture turning away from language, from clarity, from complexity, from the liberal arts and our best educational traditions. From "illumination" in every form. The false populism that has empowered the Republican Party is anchored unashamedly in anti-intellectual prejudice, in rejecting an "elite" identified with erudition and expertise. The same spirit dominates social media, with their legions of furious flesh-eating "trolls" and volcanoes of uninformed and misinformed opinion. The novelist Jonathan Franzen expressed his frustration in a recent interview: "The internet is all about destroying the elite, destroying the gatekeepers. The people know best. You take that to its conclusion, and you get Donald Trump: 'What do these Washington insiders know? What does the elite know? What do papers like *The New York Times* know? Listen, the people know what's right.'"

It's no rhetorical flourish to assert that this all-American brand of "populism" privileges, sanctifies, and literally enthrones Ignorance. It disrespects education, creativity, originality, and taste; it's a poisonous influence on the arts and on all our cultural artifacts. Dante's living descendants, serious American writers like Franzen whose books can no longer compete with James Patterson's, are beginning to articulate their distress. Richard Russo has written that a novel like his *Empire Falls* (2001), published today, "would have to be set in a tribal America that has stopped listening, that may have little interest in a novelist's musings." And consider America's once-illustrious film industry, now devoting most of its energies and financial resources to grindingly stupid superhero sequels—squads of embarrassed actors in tights and belted underpants, playing airborne mutants who vanquish various avatars of Dr. Evil. I've been told that several important "intellectuals" are addicted to Marvel Comics superheroes, and I'll regard that as the intellectual equivalent of the bubonic plague until someone can explain it for me.

In the annals of irony, my epiphany in Dante Park is a gift that keeps on giving. Dante and his contemporaries had ample darkness to deal with— endless local wars and factional bloodshed, an entrenched Catholic Church with its inquisitors burning heretics and its religious orders that had monopolized and censored intellectual activity for centuries. Not to mention a real bubonic plague, the Black Death that killed half the people in Europe a few years after Dante's death. But there's no question that they believed, from the thirteenth century forward, that they were emerging from the Dark Ages and generating light for a brighter day to come. For artists and scholars who laboriously copied ancient manuscripts and wrote millions of words with quill and ink in longhand, the concept of "information destruction" would have seemed as bizarre as gender reassignment or animal rights. At the time Dante died, the Republic of Florence was supporting six elementary schools and four high schools with more than ten thousand students. The high schools taught literature and philosophy, and it's even recorded that a few of their students were girls.

Seven centuries later in America, a republic with infinitely more wealth and a much higher technical rate of literacy, only the most stubborn optimist could overlook the intellectual stagnation and cultural dry-rot that make another Dark Age seem possible, if not imminent. Notable journalists, experiencing scorn and bewilderment, are writing books with titles like *The Death of Truth* by former *New York Times* book reviewer Michiko Kakutani.

In a benighted age, Dante was one of the first to understand that language is the essential battleground of civilization. A fluent Latinist, he wrote his greatest poetry in the Tuscan vernacular, to expand the reach and influence of "those who know." His scholarly Latin treatise "De vulgari eloquentia" is a masterwork of modern philology, defending the vernacular and probing the nature, origins, and purpose of language. An Italian American, the novelist Don DeLillo, was our first prominent writer to sound an alarm about the rapid degradation of public language and its dire consequences.

In *White Noise* (1985), he bemoans an American landscape of "abandoned meanings." The central conflict in another DeLillo novel, *The Names* (1982), is between characters who represent the holy and the profane uses of language—as a means of opening up this bright world we've been gifted, or as a means to control it. A character in *The Names* says, "Language is the River of God."

That's a sweet theology few subscribe to, in the consumer society where American English is beaten mercilessly from dawn to dusk, where cell phone texts and 140-character things called "tweets" are the new lingua franca, where "information destruction" is a respectable vocation. If language is civilization's critical battleground, the philistines and cynics, the inarticulate and proud of it like the president, have been winning many skirmishes—and perhaps some major battles—against the forces of light. Who can say whether the tide of battle is reversible? When Dante and Boccaccio struggled against an uncooperative Church to expand the community of "those who know," could they have comprehended a community, numbered in the tens of millions, who don't know, don't wish to know, and don't wish to hear from those who do? What sort of people will be walking by the poet's statue, if it's still standing there on Broadway fifty years from today?

The Twilight of Truth?

2017

The most baleful mischiefs may be expected from the unmanly
conduct of not daring to face truth because it is unpleasing.
—THOMAS ROBERT MALTHUS

What person do they elevate
above the storm cloud's smoking wrath,
even above the stars, or fate?
—The one who brings the world the truth.

—And who is heartlessly consigned
to fog and darkness, in sackcloth
to freeze in mud and icy wind?
—The one who brings the world the truth.

—VASILY KAZANTSEV, *Who Has Been Exalted*,
translated from the Russian by Henry Taylor

F ew of us in the news media ever expected to live in a country where
millions of benighted citizens go shopping for their reality, for designer "truths," much as they go shopping for designer furniture or
fashions. Or where the most successful salesman of custom-tailored reality,
a macabre fugitive from the slime pits of reality television, could become
an American president with the insufferable gall to call the most respected
American journalists and media "the enemy of the people."

The forty-fifth president is not a learned man, which is possibly the
greatest understatement I ever committed to print. He can't be expected to
know what Thomas Jefferson, a very learned man (and a natural redhead)
who once represented the government of the United States, had to say on
this subject: "Were it left to me to decide whether we should have a government without newspapers or newspapers without a government, I should

not hesitate to prefer the latter." Donald Trump certainly never heard what
the late I. F. Stone, a more recent patriot who represented the press, had
to say in support of Jefferson's choice: "With a free press, if the government does something wrong, it will become known and the government
can fix it. But if something goes wrong with a free press, the country will go
straight to hell."

It's no surprise that a population coarsened by rhetorical overkill, by
campaign crowds screaming, "Lock her up!" last year at every mention
of Hillary Clinton, failed to mobilize in furious defense of the free press
and the First Amendment. But every reporter and editor, every lawyer and
judge, every historian recognized immediately that this "enemy" business is
nothing like business as usual. In a classroom at Columbia University fifty
years ago, I heard the distinguished historian William Leuchtenburg deliver a lecture titled "The Press and the Presidency," illuminating the colorful, often adversarial relationship between the White House and the Fourth
Estate. The other night I drank a glass or two with Dr. Leuchtenburg, now
a still-productive ninety-four, and received his reassurance that no, never
had any previous president been stupid (he may have said "naive") enough
to declare himself in hostile opposition to the entire news establishment.

The closest analogy to Trump's declaration of war on the newsroom
came at the very beginning of the American experiment, in 1798, when
John Adams and his Federalist-controlled Congress passed the Alien and
Sedition Acts, and several newspaper editors actually served jail time for
unrestrained attacks on the second president. The United States was in a
very exposed and precarious position in the world, barely free of British
armies and newly alienated from France. If Adams was paranoid about
his antagonists in the press, he was not alone—George Washington supported the Sedition Act, and Adams's wife Abigail, outraged by the "criminal" language directed at her husband, had insisted on it. One great difference between 1798 and 2017 is that Adams, while in error, was arguably a
more honest, honorable, and intelligent man than most of his enemies in
the press. And America itself was only nine years old—an infant nation still
nursing at liberty's breast, not a middle-aged, supposedly mature 228. Adams's impulse was to overprotect a fragile child in dire need of postnatal
care; Trump's, apparently, is to dominate a prematurely senile democracy
by depriving it of its last links to reality.

Still more bloodcurdling than President Trump's "enemy of the people"
outburst was a speech on the floor of Congress by the Texas Republican La-

mar Smith, who advised his constituents, "Better to get your news directly from the President. In fact, it might be the only way to get the unvarnished truth." This man serves in the House of Representatives, he swore an oath to uphold the Constitution of the United States. He appears to be unaware that his speech is a clarion call for fascist dictatorship, in the words and in the mold of toadies who serve Kim Jong Un or Robert Mugabe.

What internal putrefaction has reduced us to this, to a Lamar Smith, to stone-blind partisans who take the word of a spectacular, apparently pathological liar over the collected words of an entire caste of professional journalists, most of them still committed to the idea that objective truth is the Holy Grail of their calling? The profession's commitment to the truth has varied widely, from individual to individual and from one historical period to another. A wise reader of newspapers and magazines is always a skeptical reader. But accusing America's most venerable and self-respecting media of peddling "fake news" when they contradict the president or catch him in a lie—this is groundbreaking behavior where only tyrants have broken ground before.

There was widespread mirth when presidential henchperson Kellyanne Conway described a colleague's flagrant fictions as "alternative facts." There was less when it became evident to us elitists that America sustains an enthusiastic constituency for "alternative facts" and genuine "fake news"—lies manufactured and distributed for the sole purpose of manipulating that constituency. "Alternative fact" is a perfect point of departure because it illustrates both the bad faith of partisan hacks like Conway and the fact that language is a critical battleground in this struggle for the hearts and minds of Americans. Semantically, it's an obvious oxymoron, a self-contradicting expression. There are alternative opinions, there are alternative interpretations of facts, but there are no "alternative facts." "Fact" is a word that accepts no alternatives. It means "This is the case." Any alternative is not the case. It's a misperception or a deliberate lie.

It is a demoralizing sign of cultural and linguistic collapse when we have to go digging at the roots of words like "fact" and its more glamorous, poetic sibling, "truth," to stake out a position for political debate. The human race has been searching for truth—and defining and redefining it—since long before the invention of the printing press, or any semblance of organized media. Plato and Aristotle, Confucius and the Buddha all made serious contributions to the pursuit of truth and meaning, known to philosophers as "epistemology." The Christian fathers, from Saint Augustine to

Thomas Aquinas, offered a variety of "alternative" visions. But it was only at the dawn of the age of science, in the seventeenth and eighteenth centuries, that European philosophers—prominently René Descartes, Baruch Spinoza, John Locke, David Hume, and Immanuel Kant—found the epistemological confidence to discard the received truths of their ancestors.

In spite of the opposition of the Christian Church, which realized that its power depended on a monopoly of the truth, many governments promoted science because it seemed to promise progress and prosperity. The scientific method's most notable secular enemies were the homicidal dictators Hitler and Stalin, whose captive scientists concocted strange theories to suit their masters' ideologies. For the most part science, technology, and the search for truth supported and complemented each other, through the Industrial Revolution and much of the twentieth century. And then at a certain point, and particularly in the United States with its mystical faith in capitalism, they began to betray each other.

The consumer society proved to be no friend to epistemology. Clear language, which had been one of the sharp tools of the Enlightenment, began to lose an uneven battle with advertising, a smothering cloud of duplicitous verbiage where truth was never at a premium. Technology, with the invention of television, has made advertising ubiquitous and surrounded it with cheap, disposable entertainments that distract a mass audience from more challenging cultural diversions. The cheapest and least real of all have been TV shows labeled "reality." The evil genius Roger Ailes, a disgraced sexual predator who might have been proud to be called the Joseph Goebbels of the conservative revolution, erased the line between news and propaganda with his wildly successful Fox News network. Ex–disc jockeys and Republican Party hacks impersonated journalists and experts on everything from climate science to foreign policy, and found a huge audience that could be fooled all of the time, and loved it.

That same decade, the 1990s, saw the high-water moment of a kind of feckless "relativism" in the humanities, with many postmodernist scholars arguing that historical truth is nothing but opinion, myth, and ideology. A truism—essentially "Hey, you never know for sure, Jack"—was elevated to ideology by intellectuals who should have known better. I smelled the infuriating attitude that Truth, since it was so elusive, was no longer worth pursuing, at least not by sophisticates. Absolute truth may lie well beyond the reach of our poor simian brains. But is it too much to demand absolute respect for the truth, and absolute desire to push toward it rather than away from it? If this was the gold standard, most journalists I know would out-rank nearly all of their critics.

Looking around the American marketplace, twenty years ago, you might fear that the truth had no friends at all. But the worst was still ahead. If the pursuit of objective Truth is the camel with a broken back, the internet and the twenty-first century's infernal, addictive social media were the final straw. Where there had been a few dozen news sources, many of which had honestly earned the public's trust, suddenly there were hundreds of competing, conflicting sources. And literally millions of strident voices, their motivation sinister or unknown—a host of unreliable narrators vying to tell America's story.

Exposure—hits, clicks, page views—became the measure of success instead of accuracy. The line between a journalist and a shill was blurred deliberately, and fatally. "Respectable" media struggled, with limited success, to separate themselves from the din. The best of news consumers, the truth seekers, were frustrated and confused. The worst did something terrible—terrible for truth, for free speech, for democracy. They embraced the "alternative facts" that made them most comfortable, and ignored the rest. The final ironic twist, in a culture where language is becoming a medium for manipulation instead of communication, was a president of the republic who is both a manufacturer and a devoted consumer of "alternative facts." Traditionally known as lies.

Where could honest seekers find certain truth, in this maelstrom of manipulation and misinformation? It's much easier to tell them where they won't find it. Where truth is concerned, wishful thinking is always where the red flag waves. The road to intellectual hell is paved with wishful thinking. The thing that is least likely to be true—a blissful afterlife, for instance, and forgiveness for all our sins—is the thing the believer most passionately wishes to be true. This is not a welcome caution, I know, for believers in traditional religions. But people who can will themselves to believe in angels—three-quarters of Americans claim that they do—can will themselves to believe in damn near anything.

It's hard to sustain much enthusiasm, or optimism, for a country where half the people expend as much effort hiding from the truth as Hume, Spinoza, and company expended in pursuit of it. "Three things cannot long be hidden," according to Gautama Buddha: "The sun, the moon, and the truth." But the Enlightened One never knew Roger Ailes or the Koch brothers. America produces very few followers of the Buddha, who sat under a pipal tree for forty-nine days and swore never to arise until he found The Truth. It might take even longer for a modern seeker to find it on social media.

The path to the truth was never a wide, level, well-lighted one. Undisputed facts are hard to come by; to offer anything labeled "truth" is to invite derision from both cynics and postmodernists, who ask, legitimately, "Just whose truth? Yours?" The philosophical debate over subjective reality—do any two human beings experience this world the same way?—will never be resolved. But it's easier to expose falsehood than to enshrine unchallenged truth, and there are useful rules of thumb. When many people agree on a matter of fact, and no one disagrees except those who have much to lose by agreeing, it's generally safe to believe the majority. It's possible that Bill Cosby never harmed any of those women, and possible that Roger Ailes and Bill O'Reilly (or Donald Trump) never crossed that line with their female accusers, either. It's possible that burning fossil fuels has nothing to do with global warming, though virtually all scientists disagree, and the only voices on the other side are selling fossil fuels.

Sometimes it comes down to probability—and credibility. I think it's fair to say, of my generation in the news business, that most of us have been caught in mistakes, but very few of us have been caught in lies. I was once sued for millions of dollars by a media executive who claimed I had libeled him, but a jury found otherwise. Truth, it says in libel law, is an absolute defense. Most of the journalists the president calls "enemies of the people" have never had their veracity challenged in court. The president, who's been involved in hundreds of lawsuits, has never had his veracity sustained in court, as far as I can tell. He's had it impeached nearly everywhere else, by Republican rivals, Democrats, and journalists alike. In his native New York City, no one trusts Trump and scarcely anyone voted for him—one voter in nine. "I wouldn't believe Donald Trump if his tongue were notarized," deputy mayor Alair Townsend famously warned her boss, Mayor Ed Koch, who remembered Trump as "one of the least likable people I have met during the 12 years that I served as mayor."

Blame it on dementia, sociopathy, or just a dismal lack of integrity, but a confirmed serial liar is now America's liar in chief. More disturbing than his own paranoid imagination are the poisoned sources of much of the "news" he absorbs and appears to believe. The preposterous scandals and conspiracy theories circulated by right-wing media like Breitbart and Infowars make Fox News look like *Reader's Digest*. Many of these outlaws of the airwaves and the internet—Rush Limbaugh, Alex Jones, Michael

Savage, Laura Ingraham, and company—earn millions of dollars because millions of angry, irrational Americans feed their inner fires with these fantasies. The Far Right learned long ago that its target audience requires no verification, no traditional fact-checking of any kind. And now the target audience includes the strange fact-free fellow who sometimes sleeps in the White House.

Wild characters inhabit this netherworld of misinformation. On the radio Trump's favorite, Alex Jones of Infowars, sounds like a madman raving in a padded cell. But a journalist's quarrel with the kamikaze pilots of the Right is entirely apart from the culture wars. It doesn't matter whether they're "conservative," whether I disagree with them about the role of the federal government, or the tax code, or even civil rights or reproductive rights. I loathe and fear them because they lie deliberately, and accept no responsibility when fools believe them. For them to call legitimate journalists "enemies of the people" is not the pot calling the kettle black. It's more like a charcoal briquette screaming, "Black!" at a snowball.

Two decades ago a fifty-year-old essayist, well past the high noon of his idealism, published a meditation on the nature and value of truth. Titled "Nothing But the Truth," it was his anxious response to a public moment when political propaganda had begun to masquerade as news, and one academic necromancer of the trending postmodernist tribe had gone so far as to declare that "the search for truth is meaningless." The following passage captures the spirit of that tortured writer's counterattack.

> For every lie, for every deceitful silence, some horrible crime goes unremarked and unpunished, some dreadful mistake lies waiting to be repeated. This is no daydream. This is more than your point of view, your angle of vision. It matters, profoundly, Just How It Was. Lee surrendered, not Grant. The smoke from Auschwitz carried an unbearable smell. Anne Boleyn's head was severed from her body. Between which two vertebrae the blade fell, that alone is a matter for conjecture.
>
> Who fired the first shot, how tall was the general, was it raining? It all matters. It's my conviction that cruelty follows a lie, loves a lie, makes its nest in a lie. And I've never been able to divine any purpose in our individual human lives, unless it's to reduce the sum of human cruelty during the time when we're alive. That's reason enough to press for the truth, to expose falsehood, even to deplore ambiguity if it's thick enough for cruelty to hide behind it.

Actually, that writer was me. And twenty years later, in the throes of a political and cultural decline few of us could have imagined in 1996, this idealistic flourish still rests at the core of my embattled system of beliefs. But I'm much less certain, now, that most of you are with me.

Apocalypse When?

IS REALITY MELTING WITH THE ICE CAPS?

2023

The Four Horsemen are approaching at a canter (the Fifth Horseman may be a fat man with an orange face who traded his pale horse for a golf cart). Apocalypse advances on its own schedule, and it's probably an illusion that we can do anything to fend it off or speed it up. But the summer of 2023 feels like a turning point, when those dread Horsemen may break into a gallop. July was the hottest month in recorded human history, July 6 may have been the hottest day since human beings evolved, and scientists who study sediments and ice cores calculate that those were the highest global readings in at least 125,000 years. The year 2023 is well on its way to achieving the same distinction as "hottest ever." "This would mean that nothing even remotely resembling a human civilization has ever known a world this hot," concludes Bill McKibben in *The New Yorker*.

Canada, Hawaii, and Greece are on fire, the ocean water off South Florida is now warmer than a normal human body. Vermont, half underwater, is the new Bangladesh, and heat dome–doomed Texans have been waiting for weeks to breathe any outdoor air cooler than 100 degrees Fahrenheit. Parts of the American Southwest are becoming uninhabitable. "The era of global warming has ended," declared the secretary-general of the United Nations. "The era of global boiling has begun." Climate disasters triggered by the heat—severe storms and floods—have cost struggling economies nearly $40 billion.

Global warming and drastic climate change are the central facts that will shape the future of our species and all species on this planet. Climate scientists have done their work and published their consensus. The earth is warming too rapidly, the polar ice caps are melting, and the nine billion humans who burn fossil fuels and create greenhouse gases are the villains. If this climate consensus even required one final proof, it's the infernal heat we're suffering this summer, heat that's causing thousands of deaths, destroying ecosystems as well as economies, and showing us much more than a glimpse of apocalyptic miseries that lie ahead.

We have essentially done this to ourselves. The case is closed. This is no longer a matter of opinion, of opposing ideologies or philosophies. There are no respectable scientists who dissent, no argument against the consensus that commands any respect, no politicians who can question the science without exposing themselves as prostitutes who depend on the philanthropy of the fossil fuel industry. Anyone still clinging to climate-change denial is either a liar who profits from lying or a sorry primate with the cognitive range of a zucchini. Denial has been so thoroughly discredited—and at such a terrible price—that deniers should worry about sweating, suffocating mobs that come to burn their homes.

How many summers like this one before vigilantes go after these lethal cynics and fools? Where do they live? Pick up your torch and follow me. We can start with the Heritage Foundation, the right-wing "think"(?) tank that has prepared Project 2025, a postelection Republican strategy that would roll back or eliminate every effort to reduce emissions and face up to climate change. For the Heritage crew, for the Heartland Institute, for all these whores with their hands deep in the pockets of Big Oil and Big Coal, climate change is still a "hoax" perpetrated by Joe Biden and those job-killing liberals. Is Project 2025, a $24-million war on reality, for real? Well, I read about it in *The New York Times*, which used the verb *gut* to describe the project's plans for every program that attempts to slow global warming. If you can't even imagine this level of genocidal cynicism—or genocidal ignorance—you haven't paid enough attention to the Republican Party's descent into criminal incoherence.

Heat has become the worst enemy of all living beings, the very face of the apocalypse to come. But apocalypse can wear different disguises. Most Americans who identify as journalists have made a living working for newspapers and magazines. For our shrinking tribe, the news of our profession is like a morning edition filled with nothing but obituaries. At least two newspapers die every week, and more than 2,500 have been shut down since 2005. That's a quarter of all the nation's newspapers; more than a third will be gone by 2025. Nearly 60 percent of all newsroom jobs have been lost over those last two decades, along with 70 percent of the newspaper industry's revenues. Seventy million Americans now live in "news deserts" where no local news source is available. Even cities as large as Pittsburgh and New Orleans no longer support print dailies.

This is a dirge with many verses, for many voices. The Gannett chain, which owns more than two hundred dailies in forty-three states, is now owned by a Japanese hedge fund called SoftBank, which was predictably unmoved when hundreds of Gannett journalists staged a walkout to protest shrinking newsrooms and declining standards. Another hedge fund, Alden Global Capital, specializes in buying failing dailies, slashing payrolls, and selling off assets. Legendary papers like *The Baltimore Sun* and the *Chicago Tribune* are among Alden's victims. Half of America's surviving dailies are now owned by hedge funds and private equity firms.

I have friends with Pulitzer Prizes who are essentially unemployed. Each sad story, each statistic cuts closer to the bone. The industry's great remaining powers aren't immune to the slow death of Print. *The Washington Post*, rescued from insolvency in 2013 by the Amazon megabillionaire Jeff Bezos, projects its 2023 losses at $100 million and plans layoffs. *The New York Times* recently shut down its fabled sports desk, a personal injury to lifelong readers like me who remember Red Smith, Arthur Daley, and Dave Anderson—and my grad school professor Joe Durso—with the same reverence we offered Ted Williams or Bill Russell.

The blight that's devastating printed news hasn't spared the frugal alternative end of our business, either. Here in Maine, where I hide from the summer heat, last month's demise of *The Portland Phoenix* brought down the final curtain on the family of alternative weeklies that began in 1966 with *The Boston Phoenix*, a paper I admired so much that I joined in an attempt to emulate it in North Carolina. In the same news cycle, Maine's dominant news baron, who owned *The Portland Press Herald* and a score of other dailies and weeklies, announced that he was selling the *Press Herald* and most of his other properties to the nonprofit National Trust for Local News.

The *Press Herald* sale shouldn't be mourned as more of the same, journalists will argue, because nonprofit owners like the National Trust are idealists whose mission is to rescue these local papers from hedge-fund predators and irrigate the news deserts of America. I don't dismiss that argument. But the message we can't ignore is that newsprint operations are no longer financially viable. In order to fulfill its critical role in a functioning democracy, a free press requires professionals who are not only idealistic, but experienced and adequately funded. When you can't sell ads or compete for eyeballs, your future is uncertain at best. When journalism schools have been limited to trust-fund babies and masochists taking vows of poverty, the end is near.

For print media it's late in the game, fourth down and 40. The swan song of the local newspaper isn't everyone's tearjerker. But this isn't about newsroom nostalgia, or the aging minority of news consumers who still like to hold a printed paper in our hands. It's about a population, an information culture that's rapidly losing its connection to reality, in part because it has turned its back on its most reliable guides. Public confidence in the press establishment was permanently damaged by a raging idiot of a president who called the news media "the enemy of the American people" and dismissed every story that didn't flatter him as "fake news."

In the wake of Trump's coinage, actual fake news blossomed everywhere, from the meretricious blend of news coverage and Republican propaganda on Fox News to such outrageous fountains of falsehood as Alex Jones's Infowars. This deadly toxin has even spread to local newspapers. Media watchers identify at least 1,200 local news outlets funded by right-wing activists, false neighbors who spread algorithm-generated fake news. Journalist Ryan Zickgraf compared them to "pink slime," a stomach-churning slaughterhouse by-product used to adulterate ground beef. "As traditional newspapers continue to die off," he wrote, "pink slime outlets are rapidly filling the gaps."

But it's no secret that it's new technology, the swift and chaotic digitalization of information, that has undermined traditional journalism and left it groping for its identity. History will rule on the decidedly mixed blessings of the internet. The impact of social media, on what contemporary Americans know and believe, has been predominantly dreadful. "The erosion of trust in basic facts is largely the result of too many people getting their news from social media platforms," Steven Brill of NewsGuard has stated bluntly. Brill, the founder of Court TV, is about to publish a book apocalyptically titled *The Death of Truth*. Will I have the courage to read it?

"We are living through an information revolution," Julia Angwin writes in the *Times*. "The traditional gatekeepers of knowledge—librarians, journalists and government officials—have largely been replaced by technological gatekeepers: search engines, artificial intelligence chatbots and social media feeds."

I don't know what to make of artificial intelligence, at a time when the natural intelligence of my compatriots seems to be running so thin. I know that my wizard of a son-in-law, manipulating some kind of chatbot, took only a few seconds to produce an apocryphal news story that would satisfy most editors. I've hired reporters who couldn't match it.

I'm saving the worst news for last. "Journalism is the first rough draft of history" is a quote attributed to *Washington Post* publisher Phil Graham. But the final draft requires historians. In an essay titled "This Is Actually the End of History," the scholar Daniel Bessner documents the de-emphasis of history—and all the liberal arts—in American universities. Barely a quarter of 2017's history PhDs had tenure-track jobs four years later, Bessner claims, reflecting a dramatic reduction in tenured positions that has left 70 percent of America's college teachers unprotected. Undergraduates who hope to make a living avoid history, and the number of degrees earned by history majors fell by a third between 2012 and 2019. "It's the end of history," according to Bessner. "Entire areas of our shared history will never be known because no one will receive a living wage to uncover and study them."

No Herodotus, no Gibbon, no Bill Leuchtenburg (teacher, friend, centenarian) to chronicle the twenty-first century? We all know who will step up to fill the vacuum. "Who controls the past controls the future," George Orwell wrote in *1984*.

"When there are no historians to reflect meaningfully and accurately on the past, then ignorance and hatred are sure to triumph," Bessner writes. And darkness falls. A different kind of darkness, a darkness those of us who have lived in brighter times can scarcely imagine. The darkness of abysmal ignorance. And along with it this relentless heat.

The distinguished literary scholar Louis Rubin Jr. once wrote an introduction to a book of my essays, overgenerous but with one caveat, that some readers might find my pessimism depressing. No doubt he was right. But that was years ago, and I'm afraid the world has caught up to me. When there are no knights of the newsroom to slay the big dragons like Donald Trump and Alex Jones, when there are no historians to test their work and place it in context, night falls swiftly. And we can hear the hoofbeats of those ghastly Horsemen.

PART SIX

Reflections and Meditations

Otherwise Occupied

WHAT PRICE REVOLUTION?

2011

Every time a citizen with good intentions provokes a police-state reaction from the local authorities, the angels smile and society moves one millimeter closer to salvation. It doesn't take much to provoke them. Just down the road in liberal, affable Chapel Hill, where I lived for twenty-three years without experiencing police brutality or much civil disobedience either, a reporter with a camera recorded steroidal officers in full SWAT-team battle gear, pistols and assault rifles at the ready, charging an unarmed encampment of self-described anarchists who had "liberated" a vacant building. A few seconds later the reporter was arrested, handcuffed, and forced to lie face down on the pavement with the unfortunate anarchists, who had neither resisted nor threatened any crime greater than trespassing. Amazed bystanders chanted, "Shame! Shame!"

Shame, indeed. Attempts by the police chief and the mayor to defend this preposterous cinematic overkill only added to the embarrassment. They claim that the assault rifles were not aimed at the protesters, but the photograph is there for everyone to see that they're lying. Police attacked without warning due, they claimed, to "the known risks associated with anarchist groups," as if America has been much plagued by anarchist violence. If a protester had made a nervous grab for a cell phone or a fountain pen, would we have had a bullet-riddled (unarmed) corpse lying on Franklin Street? For that frozen moment caught by the beleaguered reporter's camera, downtown Chapel Hill looked like the streets of Cairo or Damascus.

This is North Carolina, where we like to believe that our law enforcement officers still emulate Sheriff Andy Taylor of the canonical Andy Griffith Show. What would Andy have done in the same situation, instead of recruiting fifteen commandos in riot gear to arrest seven unarmed trespassers? He would, of course, have sent over Aunt Bee with a plate of fresh brownies, and then amiably advised the young people that they could have breakfast tomorrow at home, or with him at the jailhouse—their choice. And he would have kept his excitable deputy Barney Fife, with his one bullet, as far from the crime scene as possible.

Real life was never much like *Mayberry R.F.D.* But Chapel Hill is nothing much like Oakland or Manhattan, where a wild variety of dangerous characters might be camping out with the idealists. I'm sympathetic to the plight of police officers, who, thanks to America's psychotic gun cult and its captive legislators—next to suicide bombers, the craziest people left on earth—face the *Streets of Laredo* every day on the job. Last week in Wake County, a deputy answering a domestic disturbance call took a shotgun blast in the chest and was saved only by his bulletproof vest. In the NRA's Second Amendment Nation, any gray-haired lady tending her philodendrons may be packing a Glock. But in a temperate zone like Chapel Hill, someone in authority ought to be experienced and prudent enough to realize that college-town demonstrators are a fairly harmless lot compared to wife beaters, or even Tea Party soldiers whose T-shirts say "God, Guns, Babies."

"Anarchist" is one of those alien-sounding words that make simple people very nervous. Sometimes I wish that protesters would merely state their grievances and leave all those "isms," those media-tortured labels, at home. It only takes one nervous rifleman, maybe one who grew up hearing about depraved radicals and atheists on right-wing radio, to panic and trigger Kent State, or Tahrir Square. With the Occupy Wall Street (OWS) movement now spreading to hundreds of cities and campuses, and mounting pressure on thousands of defensive and unsophisticated police officers, it would be the safe and civilized decision to leave those assault rifles back in their lockers—at least until someone spots a demonstrator carrying one, too. The liberators of the derelict auto dealership in Chapel Hill were acting independently of the local Occupy encampment, which disavowed their action while acknowledging their affiliation with the movement. But the Occupiers, whose critique of America emphasizes its mindless materialism, are no doubt delighted to point out what a sleepy Southern town full of PhDs will do to protect abandoned property. Never mind the rhetoric. Just look at the picture.

Occupy 6, Chapel Hill 0. No need to kick the extra point. Other critical points for the movement were scored at Cal Davis, where passive protesters were callously and viciously pepper-sprayed, and at Cal Berkeley, where Robert Hass, a former U.S. poet laureate, described a cordon of Alameda County deputies with billy clubs smashing students and faculty indiscriminately. Hass himself was hit in the ribs and arms, his wife was knocked to the ground, and a Wordsworth scholar was dragged across the grass by her long humanist hair. Idiot force has been deployed against Occupy at dozens of its tent cities, although assault rifles have yet to appear anywhere other than Chapel Hill. Every image of belligerent overreaction to a nonviolent protest—diligently videotaped, instantly online—is a victory for this promising experiment in civil disobedience, which in the digital age of the World Wide Web commands an audience inconceivable to Mohandas Gandhi or Martin Luther King. But those great martyrs of nonviolence, who succeeded in spite of the violence they failed to survive, laid down the rules of this game. It's about self-control—you conquer by conquering yourself. Your enemies are exposed, isolated, and in the end defeated by their own brutality and lack of restraint.

That's all to the good, unless those are your ribs, your hair. The other lesson young rebels learn rapidly is that revolutions, in the words of one of Chapel Hill's declared anarchists, "are not like a dinner party." Civil disobedience is no walk in the park. It involves serious physical risks. There are sometimes martyrs. Pressed sufficiently, even the most benign authority will usually show its fangs. Television deceives. Was there ever a real-life lawman like Sheriff Andy Taylor, who never met a malefactor he didn't like? Or even one like Marshal Matt Dillon, who was always fair and avoided violence if he could? It's not a great secret that most people who seek authority, or defend it, fall toward the controlling side of the psychological spectrum. They tend to prize order and orderly citizens, an equilibrium that civil disobedience so rudely violates. "Disturbing the peace" is a punishable offense with deep historical roots.

Disturb their peace and they will bite you, they will beat you. They might shoot you. Expect no smiles, no brownies. You make a stern, life-altering commitment when you take your grievances to the street. I had to grin at an email an old friend forwarded to me, from his daughter in New York who joined last week's night march across the Brooklyn Bridge to reclaim Zuccotti Park. "Being a revolutionary is cold work," she reports.

It's cold, dangerous, and not always rewarding. Failed movements make cynics of young people who embrace a cause with everything they have and see it come to nothing. My generation, the one that marched against segregation and the war in Vietnam, can point to major achievements and major disappointments. On our worst days we feel that we, as a generation, are a major disappointment. It's a right-wing canard that the tie-dyed Aquarians all ended up in pinstripes—true Jerry Rubins are rare—but how did the egalitarian dreams of the sixties decay into the grim corporate feudalism that Occupy Wall Street so quixotically confronts? At what point, exactly, was it clear that greed had trumped altruism and cash had devoured representative democracy? If this is a revolution we're watching, perhaps it's not so much class warfare as generational warfare. The most deluded members of my generation join the mock revolution they call the Tea Party, funded by fascist billionaires, scripted by the usual talk-radio gargoyles and apparently so stunted by the brain plaque of advancing age that it imagines the government is its archenemy, to the great amusement of the corporate leviathans who operate that government like a hand puppet.

This cruel farce draws most of its recruits from my own demographic group, and I'm ashamed. Who knows why expired testosterone leads to big guns, silly hats, and prayer breakfasts? The late George Kennan, a brilliant diplomat and historian but a disturbing elitist, once espoused limiting the vote to white males. In America's best interests, I'd be willing to see that Kennan doctrine reversed—take the vote away from white men, or at least all white men over forty-five. See what that would do for the GOP. Naturally, I hope the young people in charge would make exceptions for me and a couple of my friends. The truth, in spite of all the graybeards who keep running for president, is that our time is over. If I slept out on the ground my arthritis would cripple me. And in all honesty, though I joined a march or two in my time, passive resistance was never one of my strengths. If some storm trooper with a truncheon steamrollered my wife the way Robert Hass's wife was steamrollered, I'd get his badge number and probably burn his house down. It's an ethnic tic. You probably saw *Braveheart*.

It's up to them now, the green, clean, unexpected revolutionaries one Manhattan office worker called "those terrific kids in the park." It's up to you, whoever you are, and encouraging polls indicate that most Americans don't buy the predictable smears from the right-wing coven, the ones that dismiss you as spoiled children of privilege who would rather demonstrate than work. If our self-esteem is based on the noxiousness of our enemies—I cherish mine—you should all be swollen with pride. You've been called "fascists" by Karl Rove, a criminal thug who belongs on Cellblock B instead of Fox News. Ann Coulter claims that America views you with "hilarity and revulsion," which pretty accurately sums up her own impact and her career. "Go get a bath right after you get a job," snarls Newt

Gingrich, an influence peddler who's had no legitimate job for fifteen years and exists only to give the word "hypocrisy" a human face.

My sympathies are obvious. What you in the tents can accomplish remains to be seen. But what I think I see, through the media fog of polarized America, is the return of the full-fledged idealists (as opposed to single-issue idealists) who seemed to go underground around 1980, possibly because the mass media abandoned them during the mudslide of self-celebration that began with Reaganism and culminated in Facebook. I say God bless them, and God will if he still has any investment in the United States of America. The Goliath they challenge has crushed a thousand Davids. The good news is that "the kids" are right on target. Their diagnosis is bull's-eye correct, and the patient is critical. For this country to survive, it must find saner ways to pursue and distribute wealth, and find them quickly. The cannibal capitalism that produced a Goldman Sachs and a Bernie Madoff is subhuman and obscene. There's no form of government more inherently offensive than plutocracy—only theocracy comes close. When citizens come of age in a plutocracy, they have no moral choice but to slay Pluto or die trying.

Pluto, the Greeks' god of the underworld, doesn't equate directly with the Christians' Satan, even though one of his other names was Hades. Plutus, the Greek god of wealth, is the more obvious source of these words, though the etymology is complicated. The history of American plutocracy is shockingly simple. The Industrial Revolution fueled the metamorphosis of capitalism into a ravenous monster that devoured resources, landscapes, and human beings on a scale no wars or natural disasters had ever approached. The wealth generated by this devastation created colossal corporations and financial operations far more powerful than elected governments; long ago the individuals who controlled these giants learned that it was cost-effective to buy up the politicians and turn governments into virtual subsidiaries. Along with the unprecedented wealth of the new ruling class came two protective myths, transparently false but widely accepted: one, that the feeble, compliant federal government was somehow the enemy of free enterprise; two, the outrageous trickle-down theory, which urged us to choke the rich with riches in the hope that they would disgorge a few crumbs for the peasants.

Investment banks and hedge funds were designed as perfect engines for multiplying the assets of the affluent. The Wall Street elite of the twentieth century—Masters of the Universe, Tom Wolfe called them—flew so far above the laws of the land that they began to imagine themselves exempt from all laws, including economics, physics, and averages. This magical thinking came to a head with a wave of death-defying speculation in mortgage-backed securities, and quite suddenly, in 2008, the walls came tumbling down, exposing a phantom economy based on nothing but arrogance and sleight of hand.

Huge banks failed while others begged for taxpayer bailouts, the markets reeled and contracted, unemployment soared, foreign banks and governments began to look askance at America's credit. Instead of a stable economy and an affluent society, we confronted a hemorrhaging scandal, a crime accurately portrayed as the looting of America. We woke up from our consumer coma to discover that the bastards had stolen everything. You've seen the numbers: The wealthiest 1 percent of Americans, the superrich targeted by OWS, emerged from this shattered, looted economy with a net worth greater than the "bottom" 90 percent. In the past thirty years they've nearly tripled their after-tax income—275 percent—while the poorest fifth gained a virtually stagnant 18 percent. Economist Paul Krugman emphasizes that it's the one-tenth of 1 percent, the fabulously rich one-thousandth, who account for a lion's share of the 1 percent's gains. These high lords of lucre have increased their income 400 percent since 1979.

Meanwhile, one in seven Americans lives below the poverty line, and a full one-third—one hundred million—live in poverty or what *The New York Times* calls "the fretful zone just above it." One in fifteen, the largest percentage since the Great Depression, falls 50 percent below the poverty line, with an annual individual income under $6,000. In a recent German study that established a "social justice" index (poverty levels, education, health care, income equality) for countries in the Organisation for Economic Co-Operation and Development, the United States ranked twenty-seventh among thirty-one nations, outstripping only Greece, Turkey, Chile, and Mexico. Meanwhile, also, Wall Street banks on taxpayer life support continued to pay out billions in bonuses, monstrously inflated CEO salaries showed no signs of shrinking, and the Republican Party campaigned for more of the bloody same and a stronger dose of it—no taxes, no regulations, no unions.

This is beyond unacceptable, much closer to unspeakable—like an economic survey comparing the French court at Versailles to the sansculottes. This is not what the Founders of the Great American Experiment had in mind (they thought slavery might be the fatal worm in our apple, but it turned out to be capitalism). This is what the OWS demonstrators, emerging from our underperforming high schools and colleges, found blocking their way to the future. Critics chide them for failing to establish specific demands, but a slate of demands from Occupy Chicago struck me as savvy and dead-on—repeal tax cuts and close loopholes for the rich, prosecute the Wall Street felons of 2008, separate commercial lending from investment banking, rein in lobbyists, eliminate corporate personhood, and overturn the Supreme Court's *Citizens United* decision of 2010.

This last demand is perhaps the most critical. The decision that defined campaign contributions as free speech, delivered by the Court's 5–4 Republican majority, removed the last legal obstacles to a wallet-based political system that leaves the one or .01 percent in unchallenged control of our fortunes and our public lives. It unleashed the full lethal potential of the K Street lobbies—"Cross Us and Our Cash Will Bury You," was the *Times'* headline over its story on the *Citizens United* decision. It opened the floodgates for a multibillion-dollar campaign to defeat President Obama, and any candidates who might resist corporate feudalism, in 2012. In the words of the late Molly Ivins, "We either get the money out of politics or we lose the democracy."

There's a grave possibility that it has already been lost. But those "terrific kids" in the tents, with their black-and-blue ribs and their eyes red from pepper spray, seem to be the only Americans who are dead sure what's at stake. "I want us to be the country's moral touchstone, its unofficial conscience, its model for what is good," said one rebel named Katie, coughing with bronchitis from sleeping out. Wear garlic against the pundit or politician who sneers at Katie. She and her friends may be the last best hope, if hope there is. Join them if you're young and tough enough, send them money if you can still afford it, but for god's sake listen to them. Their voices represent either America waking up at last, or its final, futile protests about to be smothered by dumb money and dumb force. Will you sit on the sidelines and watch?

The Forever Queen

GOODBYE TO ALL THAT

2022

The Queen has died. She's no longer among the living. I struggle to imagine a dramatic corollary, a sudden absence on anywhere near the same scale. A Parisian wakes up, rubs his eyes, and sees nothing but blue sky where the Eiffel Tower stood yesterday. An Egyptian drives south from Cairo and finds nothing but shifting sands—and rental camels—where the great pyramids stood yesterday and a million yesterdays before.

Queen Elizabeth is no more. The Forever Queen was mortal after all. Longevity itself, especially a case as extreme and visible as hers, creates an unpredictable shock wave when it ends. A psychological landscape is profoundly rearranged. She was the queen when I was seven years old and when I was seventy years old, queen when I was a child and when my child had her children, queen when my mother was thirty-five and when my mother died at ninety-five. Of all the constants in the lives of people my age—war, prejudice, political stupidity, metastasizing inequality—the reign of Elizabeth Regina was by far the most benevolent. She was always there, and it took a stubbornly mean-spirited person to despise her. I'm not British; it's unlikely that I would (or could) stand for twenty-four hours in a five-mile-long line to view the Queen's coffin, as thousands of her subjects are standing as I write this. Yet respect must be paid.

Of course we never met, the Queen and I. (Though family legend has it that I met her first prime minister. As my mother told it, Winston Churchill was walking through the Public Gardens with his entourage, on a wartime visit to Halifax, when he encountered my parents pushing a pram. Noting my father's American naval uniform, the great man greeted them with "Hi, Yanks" and flashed his two-fingered V-for-victory sign at the infant in the carriage—at me, eight months old.) I lived in the United Kingdom long enough to understand that there was an entire branch of public relations devoted to making sure the Queen got a good press. But it seems that she usually deserved it. She played the hand she was dealt—if you think it was a great hand, you haven't thought about it enough—with stoicism and grace. She gave a century-long performance that merits our sustained applause.

I can't deny that her death has affected me, in a way that feels personal. What gives me the right to number myself among her mourners? You decide. I was born in a Commonwealth country, Canada, to American parents, courtesy of the Second World War. I was born in the Royal Infirmary in Halifax, Nova Scotia. All my ancestors came from Great Britain, most of them from Scotland or Yorkshire. My great-grandmother, whom I knew well as a child, was born in Yorkshire and lived through thirty-eight years of Queen Victoria's reign and the first five years of Queen Elizabeth's. Through seventy-five years in America her North-Country British accent never changed. When I was a boy and she was a widow in her eighties and nineties, she would fix me tea with milk and tell me about Victoria—"my wee queenie"—and life in horse-and-buggy England. Downstairs her son and his wife—my grandparents—had decorated their dining room with portraits of all the British queens, even Bloody Mary in a dark corner over the silver chest.

You get the picture. I ingested a much stronger dose of the Union Jack than the average faculty brat from upstate New York. And there's more. My first preteen enthusiasm was collecting stamps, and there was Elizabeth's postal face on page after page in my stamp album—St. Kitts-Nevis, Guiana, New Zealand, Ceylon, Tanganyika—remember Ceylon and Tanganyika? It was always her classic pose in profile, a woman's portrait that transcended region, that must have been seen by more human beings than any other in history. At that time the Commonwealth/Empire included nations on every habitable continent, with many islands in between.

Years later, when I was a graduate student in Edinburgh, Elizabeth's image was on every coin in my pocket and every pound note in my wallet. For a couple of years I never left my apartment without the Queen's face concealed somewhere on my person. That has to account for some of my sense that she was family. I didn't have to be English; we Americans speak English, my mother was an English teacher, my BA was in English literature. But I guess the clinching connection was Uncle Johnny Briar, a Yorkshire nurseryman who visited my grandparents several times when I was a child. Uncle Johnny advertised himself as "The Mum King"—as close as any of my mercantile forebears came to royalty or even nobility—and according to my parents his greenhouses provided the copious chrysanthemums for Elizabeth II's coronation in 1953.

If the story is true, and I'm sure there's no one left alive who could contradict it, I think it entitles me to a place, at least in spirit, in the endless line of mourners that wound along the Thames. Not a dry eye in London Town, they say. Even if you're a deep skeptic when it comes to the royal family, you have to admit that bringing the Queen's favorite pony and two of her corgis to the funeral was a nice touch.

In spite of the nostalgia I'm confessing, I'm very far from a monarchist or even an Anglophile. The English with their stubborn caste system and their fetish for glitter and pageantry aren't everyone's cup of tea (I couldn't resist that). I admit to a certain American, proletarian aversion to ultraposh accents on the BBC news feed, and I always took a dim view of the kind of American who practically falls to his knees when he hears an Oxbridge accent. I was once lucky enough to hear Sir Peter Ustinov mock every variety of that rarefied English with perfect pitch—and then turn his uncanny mimic's ear on the Americans at the table.

A colleague of mine was such an Anglophile that I used to refer to his infatuation as Anglophilia. He was an officer of an organization called the English-Speaking Union, and he never passed up a chance to bring some prominent Englishman to Raleigh, North Carolina. On any number of occasions I walked into his office and found him deep in conversation with Sir This or Lord That. I'm afraid I treated his enthusiasm satirically. Though I've had close friends who were Brits, none were knighted and none were Tories. In Edinburgh my closest associates were from the hardcore Labor Left, including a couple of Trotskyites. They were limited in their enthusiasm for the Queen, or even the Union.

It's not a contradiction that troubles me. You didn't have to endorse the whole package to admire the Queen. Wearing England's crown is more of a theatrical than an administrative assignment. To serve as a purely symbolic, ceremonial monarch requires patience, diplomacy, natural dignity, and unflagging commitment to the script. The beauty of Queen Elizabeth is not only that she was so good at all that, but that she was, or should be, the end of all that. The age of kings is long over. Of course poor old Charles has no choice but to stumble ahead with this venerable charade, this pretense of power where there is nothing but show. The royal family has been dismissed by its detractors as "the royal zoo," but that's too cruel. It's really more like a theme park, a very expensive one that charms foreigners more than many of the Britons who pay for it.

The best lesson from the royal Windsors is that it's always naive and reactionary to place someone on a throne, or any pedestal that implies superiority to the rest of the human race. Actual democracy begins only when the last pedestal is leveled. History might be headed in the right direction if the beloved ancient Queen on her bejeweled catafalque were the last great personage to be raised above us. Admiration is a generous emotion; idolatry, always misplaced, is usually dangerous. Every cult of personality, whether it's built around a monarch, a self-declared prophet, a religious or political demagogue, or a celebrity entertainer, is sustained by a childish, archaic belief in giants, in supermen and less often superwomen.

There are no such things as superior races or noble bloodstreams. Belief in them is a throwback to an early-adolescent phase of human development, when might made right, ignorance was general, and awe was so much easier. When it comes to lust, envy, vanity, malice, and selfishness, we are all cut from the same flawed cloth, burdened by the same temptations. Some of us try hard to resist the darker parts of our nature, some don't try hard enough, some don't try at all. Scandals have plagued the royal family and tormented the Queen, but I doubt that Cheatin' Chuck and his brother Randy Andy were much different from other rich twits of their generation. They were the ones who had to live in a fishbowl. You have to get used to the British media to understand what a crazy fishbowl it is, and what a strange institution the imaginary monarchy has become.

Two of history's most powerful forces, religion and nationalism, almost invariably trace their roots to cults of personality—and they've caused more violent deaths than any other forces in human memory. We need to move on. We need to remember the Queen in two ways, as an excellent individual and as the embodiment of a poor idea. She was an ordinary woman, by most accounts, who found herself in an extraordinary situation and exceeded all expectations. As a royal princess she began her life with respect she hadn't earned, and she went on to earn a great deal more. But she was an anachronism, a holdover from another world where people with good sense believed in things like "royal blood" and the divine right of kings.

"We will not see her like again," declared Scottish First Minister Nicola Sturgeon, fair praise that cuts in both directions, from the leader of a subnation where half the natives want out of the UK as soon as possible. We can honor the Forever Queen with good conscience, and still bid a polite farewell to the world of imperial illusions that made her possible.

Out of Date

THE JOYS OF OBSOLESCENCE

2014

The word itself looks weird and ancient, like something indecipherable scrawled on a cave wall or half-eroded from a decrepit tombstone. The word is "crwth," a Welsh word—in English, where vowels rule, the word became "crowd." The Irish version is "cruit." The musical instrument that goes by these names is as archaic as the lovely Welsh language, and more obsolete. It's a six-string bowed harp or lyre, something like a fiddle until you hear it, that has been traced back to eleventh-century Byzantium. The crwth has been played very little, if at all, since the seventeenth century; its history is so obscure that the principal authority cited by Wikipedia is Musical and Poetical Relicks of the Welsh Bards, published by Edward Jones in 1784. If you Google "crwth," you'll find this sentence, which more or less defines obsolescence: "Since the art of crwth-playing died out so completely, and since it was an instrument of the folk culture rather than part of the academic musical world, the exact manner—if, indeed, there ever was one exact manner—in which the instrument was traditionally played, like the tunings employed, will probably never be known for certain."

A modest revival of interest in the crwth, part of the original instruments movement, is based largely on conjecture and experimentation. Elsewhere on the internet you can find a video of Sean Folsom—a rubicund American musician who bills himself as Sean the Piper—wearing a Renaissance gown and one of those flat guildsman's hats that looks like a meat pie with a velvet ribbon, solemnly playing and patiently explaining the crwth. Its sound is fetching in a way, at least to me, but distinctly . . . medieval. At this point I confess what may be obvious, that my surname, Crowther, means crwth player. Crwthist? I'm descended, at some point lost in time, from a musician who played songs now forgotten ("The repertoire of surviving crwth tunes is very small") on an instrument no one now alive knows for certain

how to play. Perhaps generations of these forlorn bards roosted in my family tree. People with surnames like Miller or Shoemaker, or the even more
antiquated Cooper or Fletcher, remind us in a similar way of lost trades and
traditions. But the Crowthers, as I see it, boast the most obsolete pedigree
of all. Even the Flintstones seemed less out of date.

As a senior citizen with arthritis and cataracts, peering myopically down
the smoking barrel of the twenty-first century, I know that bearing an expired name and representing an extinguished heritage has helped me to
understand my life and accept the arc of my own fortunes. I'm no stranger
to obsolescence. For twenty-five years I earned a living with an instrument
now consigned to an oblivion even more complete than that of the crwth,
because there will be no attempt to resurrect the typewriter. Yet this humble
machine produced a comforting music of its own. Each year, inevitably and
sadly, there are fewer of us who remember the companionable percussion
of the Royal, the Olivetti, the Smith Corona. The atonal but almost synco-
pated symphony of a big-city newsroom with its clicks and taps and ringing
carriages, its tempo as varied as the speed and vigor of the fifty typists, was
a sweet sound that will never be heard again on this planet, except in the fit-
ful dreams of old reporters.

Grim electronics and grimmer economics brought an end to all that. But
it's idle nostalgia to grieve for the tools of yesteryear. Technology has its way
with every profession, more often for the best. Lumberjacks with chainsaws
rarely yearn for those crosscut saws their fathers strained to pull; modern
fishermen don't dream of hauling nets by hand. It may be sheer coincidence
that the rapid disappearance of the typewriter and the rapid decline of journalism seem to coincide. That journalism has declined woefully is a very
easy argument to document and sustain, but not without offending sincere
individuals whose livelihood depends on its survival, in some as yet unde-
termined form.

I don't blame young people for tuning out when a bitter graybeard
evokes the good old days. Right or wrong, prescient or senescent, it's an
unbecoming role he's playing, one I'd rather avoid. Mine is a personal,
not a cultural, lament. Anyone who hasn't registered the alarming divorce
of broadcasting and professional journalism is simply very young. Yes, I
can remember when foreign bureaus and documentaries—and thoughtful objectivity—were the pride of network news departments, and the cable news Punch-and-Judy was less than an embryo. As for print journalism, which seems to be following the Smith Corona into oblivion, volumes

have been published, and will be published (for your Kindle?) to explain what happened to us and why. I have little to add to a front-page story by *New York Times* media columnist David Carr, who chronicled the pitiful disintegration of the once proud and powerful Tribune Company, publisher of the *Chicago Tribune* and the *Los Angeles Times*.

Carr's story, ironically published during National Newspaper Week, acquainted us with Tribune CEO Randy Michaels, a former radio shock jock assigned by billionaire Sam Zell to manage his controlling interest in the failing media giant. According to Carr, Michaels demoralized company headquarters in Chicago with a bizarre infusion of trash-radio culture—misogyny, sexual harassment, profane tirades, raunchy schoolboy humor, sleazy giveaways—that Tribune veterans could scarcely believe, far less tolerate. Carr reported that Michaels introduced himself to his new colleagues at a Chicago hotel bar by getting drunk and offering a waitress $100 to show him her breasts. "I have never seen anything like it," recalled one eyewitness, no longer a Tribune employee. Carr also claimed that Michaels and an executive cadre of his old radio cronies looted the bankrupt Tribune by paying themselves huge bonuses while the company staggered ever deeper into debt.

Michaels—forced to resign a few weeks later—is a short, fat, bottom-fed individual who looks like the carny selling cheese fries at the county fair. To call him a scumbag is a description, not an insult, since a shock jock is a professional scumbag—it's his stock in trade. Anyone who's never heard one of these baboons castrate a pig in the studio or audiotape a sex act in St. Patrick's Cathedral (both true) is a lucky American indeed. It's no secret that radio is a latrine; we wince because this repulsive huckster hired and fired newsroom personnel for two legendary newspapers that were, within recent memory, among America's most powerful and prestigious. Actually Michaels fired, mostly. More than four thousand Tribune Co. employees have been terminated since he and Zell took over in 2008. For newspapers, the hour is very late. For newsmagazines, perhaps even later. *Newsweek*, where I once labored, died a cruel death in the marketplace. It was purchased for $1 by a ninety-two-year-old stereo tycoon, now deceased, who merged it with the *Daily Beast*, a web magazine run by glitter-monger Tina Brown. ("Beastweek?" one reporter speculated.) *Time* magazine, another employer from my long-ago youth, has suffered similar financial and artistic decay and hangs like a decomposing albatross around Time Warner's tired neck.

The news about the news is uniformly depressing. If you're tired of hearing that from pundits and disgruntled old newshounds, take it straight from the Kansas Department of Education, which has cut off funding for high school journalism courses after a review of labor-market data. As reported in *Newsweek*, "the state deemed journalism a dying industry unfit for public funds, which are meant for 'high-demand, high-skill or high-wage jobs.'" Ouch. It's only Kansas, but it stings. To make the rout more poignant, the first jobs eliminated by the stressed-out, stripped-to-survive print media were the very jobs I used to work. Columnists, book editors, film, drama, and fine arts critics—along with investigative reporters, foreign and Washington correspondents, and editorial cartoonists—were dismissed as highbrow luxuries for newsrooms trying to get a grip on grassroots America. If I should have the good luck to live another twenty years, I suppose my résumé will provoke as much bewilderment among my grandchildren as if I'd told them I was an itinerant crwth player. They'll nod and give me a cup of something warm and pat me on my trembling shoulder. ("He said he 'reviewed' books and films for newspapers. Yesterday he muttered something about 'Pogo' and 'Li'l Abner.' Has mama checked his medications?")

But that's in 2030, when we'll all be living underground to escape the heat, and half a billion Americans will own three billion guns. (Not much hunting underground, but lots of stress to trigger domestic disputes.) My guess is that the information revolution will not be a major issue in 2030. I'm trying to process my obsolescence here in 2011, in my first year of eligibility for Medicare. The shock of having spent my professional life in "a dying industry" isn't necessarily the most traumatic assault on my sense of self. No one who wasn't in the work force—or in the world—in 1985 can possibly comprehend the speed or the magnitude of the technological metamorphosis we have just witnessed. Rip van Winkle would have had to sleep two hundred years to wake to the future shock you'd experience if you'd only been napping since the Reagan administration. Those of us who were at midlife or beyond when the cyber-tsunami struck faced adjustment pressures unlike any in human history.

How did I cope? There's an analogy that appeals to me. Here in Maine where I'm writing, we're menaced by a pack of homicidal drivers, usually males under thirty in big new trucks, who cruise narrow two-lane roads at NASCAR speeds, day or night. If you drive at conventional speed, the cowboy comes up behind you so fast the hairs stand up on your neck. If there's no sane chance for him to pass you, as is often the case on these roads, you have two choices: You can speed up dangerously to increase the distance between your bumper and his, or you can signal a right turn and pull over on the shoulder to let him streak by. The first few times I saw this second maneuver, I wondered whether it represented courtesy or terror. But it is, of course, the right move, even if it goes against your grain. And it's the move I chose, a few years ago, to accommodate the alien technology that came roaring up in my rearview mirror at one hundred miles per hour. I didn't hit the accelerator, though by nature I'm more combative than acquiescent. I pulled off the road and let the monster roll on by. Just where it's going, no one knows and I don't care.

Once you pull over, you forever wear the big "O" for obsolete. You can't hide it. The wired world snickers, your children roll their eyes, preadolescents with fists full of gadgets regard you with wonder, with pity. You become selectively illiterate, because the technology constantly spawns new words and acronyms you have no need or wish to learn. How painful is this excommunication, this life in the ghetto of the left-behind? Personally I like it here. The company and conversation are first-rate, even if most of the neighbors are drawing Social Security. The experience of dropping out of the tech rat race reminds me of a line in one of my wife's best novels, about a mountain girl in her teens who finds herself pregnant and alone, "ruint" for good according to her parents and her community. A good reputation and a good marriage are now out of reach, but she finds it mysteriously liberating. "When you're ruint," Ivy says, "It frees you up some."

When you're out of date and committed to it, it frees you up some. I honestly doubt that I'll live to regret it. The parade goes by, and it can be highly entertaining as long as you don't have to march, to learn the cadence and keep up the pace. You pick a choice seat on the reviewing stand and watch, unencumbered by performance anxiety, status, or public opinion. You don't count any more, as the marchers reckon it, and as Janis Joplin once sang in "Me and Bobby McGee," "Freedom's just another word for nothin' left to lose."

Loneliness and self-pity aren't major problems when your obsolescence is more or less voluntary. Smugness—unearned self-congratulation—is more of a threat. I hate to sound smug. I realize I'm very fortunate—blessed—to have had the option to say no. There are talented journalists my age and even older, discarded by the dying industry, who are blogging, friending, and Twittering themselves to exhaustion, hoping to catch the last seat on a train that's already disappearing down the tracks. The loss of their self-respect is a personal tragedy; the loss of their gifts and experience is a national one. And of course the option of a life off the grid was never open to Americans who began their careers post-Gates, post-Jobs, post–Silicon Valley. We live in an age when even shepherds and forest rangers are probably wired from hat to boots.

The electronic express keeps rolling, and there's no turning back. "Reject it," prescient advice Sven Birkerts offered to conclude his Luddite manifesto *The Gutenberg Elegies* (1996), now sounds as dated and wistful as the fight song of a team that lost 70–0. Yet those of us doomed to anachronism by technology enjoy many compensations, not the least of them the knowledge that we're gravely underestimated by cybersophisticates who pity us. The rumor that I've been reduced to tears and profanity by the multiple remotes that control hotel TV sets is not entirely unfounded. Mr. Wizard I am not. But the myth that computers and allied appliances are simply too complicated for tired old minds is based on the youthful assumption that everyone wants to learn this stuff, that everyone would if they could. The truth is that nearly everyone can if they have to. When circumstances force us to operate these impudent twenty-first-century machines, we fossils engage reluctantly but rarely fail. Survival-level computer skills are no neuroscience, nor were they meant to be. A motivated chimpanzee can do this, or even Randy Michaels.

It's not so hard to teach an old dog new tricks—not if his dinner depends on it. But the more tricks he has to turn to fill his bowl, the more he's going to hate you. And you can double the hatred—I speak for an incorrigible minority of old dogs—if he thinks most of your new tricks are stupid. The vices and virtues of the all-wired world merit ferocious cultural debate, but it's hard to sustain a dialogue with young people who've never lived without the glowing screens, the blinking lights, the voices from the ether. Terms of discourse have changed as rapidly as hardware and software, and created the most prodigious generation gap in history. Rising generations—as opposed to sinking ones like mine—can't be expected to grasp how quickly it happened, how it never evolved but exploded. Children born in Nagasaki after 1945 might have the same difficulty forming a clear picture of their city before the bomb. We, the obsolete, are obliged to argue from general principles. The purpose of technology is to make it easier to perform the essential tasks of our lives, tasks that include survival. But what if, instead or in addition, it merely creates tasks and problems for which there was no need, for which no human relevance can be logically demonstrated? What if it merely multiplies entities unnecessarily, in defiance of Occam's razor? How many apps does it take to screw in a light bulb?

Nielsen reports that the average teenage girl in America sends more than four thousand text messages a month, eight messages for every hour she's awake. By an admittedly rough calculation that's more social messages in thirty days than I've sent (through any and all media) in my entire life, now approaching two-thirds of a century. To me this statistic is as weird as a rumor that these girls roast and eat their pets. Apparently technology has activated some latent psychological, perhaps even genetic tendency toward incontinent interconnection, but I can't imagine what we've gained from it. There's no question that much has been lost—first and worst of all our privacy.

Privacy is the Great Divide. For the civilized—now the obsolete—it's a primary article of faith that the tougher, the more impermeable the critical membrane between public and private, the more civilization flourishes. In the past, this has been one of the few important points of agreement between serious liberals and serious conservatives, and certainly among all the Founders and architects of the republic. Without privacy there's no dignity, and without dignity "freedom" has no meaning. Thirty years ago, you could search in vain for an American who thought privacy was expendable. Yet recently one of the billionaires responsible for the rapid erosion of American privacy—some entrepreneur of the PC, cell phone, or social network industries, I can't recall—was asked how we could protect our privacy and replied dismissively, "Get over it." "Get over it," the bastard said, instantly converting my distaste and distrust to fear and loathing.

This is the grim place to which the heedless have marched us. The resistance—scattered, aging—will never produce a twenty-first-century Patrick Henry to cry, "Give me privacy or give me death." But the death of privacy, like Goya's "sleep of reason," is breeding monsters. What do we make of the handsome Indian American freshman at Rutgers, with an angelic smile and no history of antisocial behavior, who filmed and then webcast his roommate in a homosexual embrace? He never expected his victim to jump off the George Washington Bridge, but what did he expect? We'll never know what this cherubic Iago was thinking, but just as hard to understand is that webcam/computer installations are standard equipment in freshman dorm rooms. When, why did all this electronic garbage become a generational norm?

A federal court convicted Ashton Lundeby, a seventeen-year-old North Carolina high school student, of masterminding an elaborate internet scheme that involved false reports of bombs planted at universities, high schools, and FBI offices. Lundeby and his coconspirators would call in a bomb threat to the local police, record each emergency response with surveillance cameras, and then sell the footage to paying customers online. The Lundeby scheme required so much chutzpah—or criminal innocence—and so much expertise that we shake our heads in awe. But the confluence of electronic wizardry and commercial initiative is bound to remind us of billionaire Facebook entrepreneur Mark Zuckerberg and the biomovie *The Social Network* that skewered him as a tormented sociopath. I never saw *Avatar*, but Zuckerberg and many of the other creatures portrayed in *The Social Network* were far more alien to me than blue people with tails in 3D. If they are the future, please help me find the door to the past. Hand me my crwth and my bow. Put the meat-pie hat with the ribbon on my head, and point me toward a market town where someone might spare a shilling for a tune.

Criticism from the sidelines, from the happily obsolete, has been ruled inadmissible. If you don't play, who cares what you think about the players? Most of the recent books blaming psychic trauma on cyberoverload, like Jaron Lanier's *You Are Not a Gadget*, have been written by Silicon Valley apostates with second thoughts about the digital revolution. But I don't think any of us from premicrochip generations have the right to shrug and look away. We—some of us—invented, marketed, and served them this bewildering array of gadgets. And there's ample evidence that something ragged and unclean, something morally unsettling is loose among young people who could be your children and grandchildren, or mine.

Monsters whose obsessions result in crimes and lawsuits aren't isolated cases, unfortunately. They're nurtured in a flourishing internet subculture of bullies, creeps, and clowns. *The New York Times* ran a story about teenagers in an upscale suburb who were using cell phone cameras to record fights, savage beatings, and violent stunts that compete for attention on websites like Myspace and YouTube. Many of the quotes in this story by Corey Kilgannon were chilling, jaw-dropping messages from a microculture gone mad. "Kids beat up other kids and tape it, just so other kids will see it and laugh," shrugged one seventeen-year-old boy. "Or they just post stupid things they did online so other kids will look at their Web page." His friend added, "Teens always do crazy stuff but it's just that much more intense and fun when you can post it. When you live in a boring town, what else is there to do?" And another explained, "Kids put their fights online for street cred."

No less disturbing were the expert analyses the *Times* reporter solicited. "A lot of teens have this idea that life is a game and it's all entertainment," said Nancy E. Willard, who wrote a book on cyberbullying. "In doing this, they're jostling for social position and status, or establishing themselves in a certain social group, or just attracting attention. To them, this is defining who they are and what people think of them. The idea that 'people know my name' is an affirmation of who they are." A role model for many of these suburban exhibitionists was a local man whose videos of himself hurling his body through neighborhood fences, an internet sensation, spawned a national fad. "A week ago, no one knew who I was—now my name has been on every news and talk show," said this idiot, Adam Schleichkorn, now twenty-five. "I don't care that it's for something stupid. I was on Fox News cracking jokes. Maury Povich called me today. So I'm known as the fence-plowing kid. At least I'm known."

You see what I mean by divergent terms of discourse. What does a grandfather on Medicare say to the fence-plowing kid, besides "Jesus Christ, kid"? Mark Zuckerberg, the world's youngest billionaire, would be an equally tough lunch date. The infantilization of American culture seems to be an established fact—judge only from Hollywood films, which in the thirty years since I was a film critic have changed their demographic from predominantly adult to predominantly preschool. Another established fact is the link between the sedentary online life and an epidemic of obesity. But there's a chicken/egg problem with severe psychological displacement. Were Americans already evolving into strange life forms that require more and better electronic toys to mirror and exhibit themselves, or should we hold the toys responsible for their transformation?

Only the most embarrassing old-timers claim that things were better, or that we were better, way back when. To the best of my recall, teenagers of the fifties and sixties were just as cruel and status conscious and no less obsessed with sex, though we knew a great deal less about it. Adolescent lives weren't better, perhaps, but they sure as hell were different, and the difference appears to be all about context, about expanding identity groups. We lived our lives for a limited audience of parents, siblings, teachers, classmates, and neighbors. It wasn't a very attentive or demanding audience, but only one teenager in a thousand—a great athlete, a beauty queen, a musical prodigy—ever imagined a wider, even a national, audience. The rest of us accepted our limitations. Academic achievements might lead to opportunities for a richer, more comfortable life later on; catching a touchdown pass or hitting a home run could be converted into immediate status and sometimes even sexual currency, coveted and hard to come by. (Forgive the male point of view—to boys like us in those days, females were another country.)

Hardwired teens of the internet era see all the world as their stage. And sometimes it is. The common dream of online performers is to "go viral" like Adam Schleichkorn, whose original fence-busting video attracted seventy thousand viewers. The most hardcore juvenile delinquent of the fifties would have been petrified at the thought of all those eyes. But now we discover a subculture where the natural need for privacy has been reversed, somehow, into a neurotic need for constant attention—attention of any kind at all. In this alternate universe it's better to be disgusting, to be a figure of fun or an object of contempt, than to be invisible. Voyeurs demand, exhibitionists deliver, then they switch chairs. Vicariousness is all.

When did people begin to think of themselves as public offerings, as products they're obliged to market and sell from cradle to grave? A typical teenager of fifty or even twenty-five years ago was alone in his locked room sulking, possibly even reading—possibly even reading something obscene. The typical (?) teenager in 2011 seems to be out filming himself to program his Facebook page or compete for attention on YouTube. This reversal is so radical, we could debate whether "personal technology," in little more than a decade, has altered America's DNA. But the eradication of privacy as a core human value doesn't account for the cruelty, for the internet's "culture of sadism" that the computer scientist Jaron Lanier decries in his book. It doesn't account for the Rutgers atrocity or subhuman video "pranks" like attacking homeless men and beating a thirteen-year-old girl—both popular attractions on websites that encourage this spreading infection.

Is it possible that expanding the community immeasurably, from the dozens to the millions, dilutes all the positive aspects of community—compassion, loyalty, mutual support, and responsibility? That as the community expands, communality contracts until dog-eat-dog rules again? With the whole anonymous world watching, at least in your imagination, do individuals lose substance, become little more than "viewers"—totaled online as "hits"—and Facebook "friends" you'll never meet? You wouldn't beat or betray a friend, but a "friend" is another matter. This is just a suggestion from the sidelines. No doubt the fence-plowing kid has a different explanation.

The blessing conferred on those whom obsolescence has claimed is that we'll never have to compete with "the kid" for the world's attention. If you will, if you do, God help you.

Of course it's a small minority of teenagers who beat up the homeless for publicity and post nude pictures of themselves online. But I'm afraid the majority is too marinated in the culture that breeds this behavior to see how grotesque and pathetic it's become. It takes perspective. If you're still able to take one step off the grid and look back, the view might shake you up, or crack you up. The dividing line between generations is laid down sharply in *The Social Network* when Sean Parker, loathsome founder of Napster, cries out in his cups, "People used to live on farms and in cities, now we'll all live on the internet!" If Parker's outburst chills you as a vision of an ultimate dystopia more depressing than *1984* or *Brave New World*—as the filmmakers intended—you're on my side of the line. If you barely notice it, you're lost on the far side.

Elsewhere the line is not so cleanly drawn. I confess that I laugh at people who buy and prize the Dick Tracy cell phones that do everything but brush your teeth and walk your dog. I also concede that I have extremely intelligent, serious, otherwise discriminating friends who poke away at the silly things with apparent fascination. These converts are not and will not be obsolete, perhaps as a matter of pride? But without dinosaurs like me to remind them, they'd forget what the old order was like. Have I disappointed them? What did I ever do to feed a suspicion I could be seduced by gadgets that invite me to gape at movies, stock reports, spreadsheets, pornography, weather maps, and email on a screen half the size of a playing card, like some gorilla mesmerized by a Christmas tree ornament? Which of us is weird?

The last question can't be answered definitively. In the few years since it opened, the high-tech superhighway—ten lanes, no speed limit— has carried most Americans far from their origins, and lured nearly all of us out of our comfort zones. But the highway is littered with accidents, too, and road signs that lead us nowhere. It's mainly an aesthetic decision, finally, to pull off the road and turn off the ignition. It's possible to remain physically and mentally vigorous thirty years after most of your contemporaries have faded away. But I believe that each of us has a kind of cultural expiration date, and there's nothing more pitiful than people who've exhausted their cultural shelf life and don't know it. Think of the sexagenarian who claims to love Eminem. How do you know when you've expired? Maybe when popular culture pushes you beyond contempt into physical nausea. I reached that place a while ago. If you're old enough to remember Jerry Ford and you're not there yet, you will be soon. Unless, of course, you're one of the shell people with no core of sensibility or belief, ever ready to hitch a ride on anything that comes your way.

This isn't a popular song I'm playing, or one you're likely to hear again. But it isn't a dirge. Or a swan song. Obsolete and unashamed, we feel like farmers who got their crops in safely before the hard rains fell. As storm clouds gather, it's a time to walk the fields of stubble with the old dog, the hearth dog, and see, as the Bible says, that it is good. Then comes a long winter musing by the fire—though spring remains a question mark. The past is a flickering daydream, the present is turning ugly, and the future belongs to no one, though the kind of heirs we might have chosen seem less and less likely to inherit. We haven't said "goodbye," we've just said "enough."

In common usage the word "obsolete" has become too pejorative. Many outdated things—Jim Crow, the Vatican, cigarettes, the two-party political system—wear out their welcome but fail to achieve extinction rapidly enough. Yet so much that's obsolete deserved a better fate. We may be the last of our kind, but we flatter ourselves that we'll be missed, perhaps even heeded more in the future than we were in the past. In my research I came across a lovely sentence in praise of the homely, ancient instrument that gave its name to my father's family. With a minor lapse of modesty, I can pretend that the author is speaking of me: "For all of its (his) technical limitations, the crwth has great charm, and is much more than a historical curiosity."